MANAGING LIBRARY OUTREACH PROGRAMS

A How-To-Do-It Manual
For Librarians

MARCIA TROTTA

*HOW-TO-DO-IT MANUALS
FOR LIBRARIES*

Number 33

NEAL-SCHUMAN PUBLISHERS, INC.
New York, London

Published by Neal-Schuman Publishers, Inc.
100 Varick Street
New York, NY 10013

Printed and bound in the United States of America

Library of Congress Cataloging-in-Publication Data

Trotta, Marcia.
    Managing library outreach programs : a how-to-do-it manual for
librarians / Marcia Trotta.
        p.   cm. -- (How-to-do-it manuals for libraries ; no. 33)
    Includes bibliographical references (p.) and index.
    ISBN 1-55570-121-3
    1. Library outreach programs--United States--Management.
    2. Public libraries--United States--Administration.   I. Title.
    II. Series.
Z711.7.T76   1993   93-7511
                                                          CIP

CONTENTS

PREFACE

Managing Library Outreach Programs is not just about "outreach" services. It is about the survival of public library services for the 1990s and beyond. American society is undergoing rapid, sweeping changes. In order to meet the changing and growing needs of our communities, it is becoming a *basic service* to reach out beyond our walls and make library services not only *accessible*, but also *relevant* to diverse populations. Library services must be shaped not just by our professional perceptions but by "customer-focused" planning. This means service that goes beyond the traditional realm of what we have offered in the past, and far beyond the clientele to whom we have offered it.

Managing Library Outreach Programs will examine those outreach services that apply to children and young adults. The experiences (mine) upon which it is largely built grew from the need to reach out to children who just were not being brought to the library. In my community (Meriden, Connecticut), there is little in the way of public transportation. The town is spread out over 24 square miles and the library is not within easy walking distance from any elementary school. A recent survey showed that more than 90 percent of the children who came to the library had to be brought there by an adult. This knowledge, coupled with the fact that 11 percent of the community is believed to be illiterate, compelled to us to look for different means of delivering traditional library services.

Today's child is growing up in a world that is quite different from the one we knew as children—whether we are 60-something or merely 30-something! The past 20 years have brought immense changes and placed enormous pressures on family structure. Adults' financial and psychological burdens are then transferred to their children. The extended family support system is no longer intact. Too many children become fearful, angry, withdrawn— lacking of the basic necessities of life that so many of us take for granted. When children do not have the basics, it usually follows that there is no one who has the time, or desire, or even the ability to read to them. Like many earlier studies, a 1985 report produced by the Center for the Study of Reading at the University of Illinois concluded that children whose parents read to them as preschoolers were likely to do better in school.[1] The library can use outreach services as a major tool in carrying out the facet of its mission that is the preschoolers' door to learning.

In Meriden, we found that we weren't reaching many of the very children who would most benefit from our services. Major causal factors were the high illiteracy rate in the minority community and location of the library in relation to the underserved areas. Important, but less obvious, obstacles were psychological factors that both intimidated and alienated underserved youths from using our services. We found that the only way to successfully integrate library services into these communities was to reach *out* to the children and their caregivers through innovative use of resources and cooperation with community leaders and volunteers. We found that with careful planning we were able to develop services that our populations needed, realized they needed, and felt comfortable using. While outreach services might be viewed as programs in themselves, sometimes they are the means to introducing and promoting library services. Personal contacts made outside the library encourage people to come to the library. They also help librarians develop expanded services to meet potential users' requirements documented during the course of outreach visits. We found that once our new users knew us and what we did, and knew that we were interested in doing it for them, they worked with us to find ways to come to the library for the full range of services available onsite.

Managing Library Outreach Programs is organized to guide you to achieving these goals in your own community. Chapter 1 looks at the historical context of outreach and discusses some of the reasons for establishing an outreach program. Chapter 2 will take you in search of hidden library patrons—how to find community members who are underserved. Then in Chapters 3, 4, and 5 we will cover ways to secure allies in the neighborhood, ways to tailor your programs to community needs, and successful techniques demonstrated by model programs. In Chapter 6 we'll discuss the kinds of staff augmentation and training you may need. Chapters 7 and 8 give you tips and guidelines to involving adults and promoting your services.

Many sources of useful materials—both printed and audiovisual—are listed in the Resource section at the end of the book. We have included many forms and checklists to assist you in planning, implementing, and evaluating the outreach services. Use the book, write in it—and make the program suitable to your community and its needs.

Go after the resources you need, and don't give up! Remember that your goal is no less than helping to create the informed, educated, and participative populace that is necessary for a democratic society to thrive. Public libraries have a social responsibility to be a part of this process. Libraries must become dynamic, culturally diverse, social and economic catalysts for their entire community—and outreach services are central to reaching that goal.

ENDNOTE

1. Richard C. Anderson, et al. *Becoming a Nation of Readers: The Report of the Commission on Reading* (Washington, D.C.: National Institutes of Education 1985).

ACKNOWLEDGMENTS

It would be impossible to thank everyone who influenced and encouraged me in my efforts to develop outreach programs in Meriden. I am especially grateful to the Trustees of the Meriden Public Library for their encouragement and support and to Directors Marion Cook and Susan Bullock who encouraged me to follow my instincts. Special thanks to the countless staff and volunteer hours that helped me carry out this vision, and to my family for understanding when I slipped on everyday things to complete this project.

1 WHY OUTREACH?

The library promotes reading readiness from infancy, providing services for self-enrichment and for discovering the pleasures of reading and learning. Programming introduces children, and adults concerned with children to a wide range of materials and formats.[1]

"We're here! We have terrific materials! We have wonderful programs! Everyone should be coming to us!" All true, at least in the great majority of libraries, and any librarian might be forgiven for feeling this way. We *know* how good our library is and would like everyone to share its riches. Nevertheless, what we know and what non-library users perceive are not usually the same thing. Who is *not* using the library? Why not? Unless we pay attention to *their* reasons for not using the library's services, we'll have libraries that are serving only a portion of the community's constituents. It is not realistic to assume that people are going to use libraries just because they are there. The library must respond to its potential patrons. In many areas that means *outreach*: bringing services out to where they are needed. The term *outreach* is easy to define, but the execution of outreach programs requires planning, commitment, connections, and energy.

HISTORY OF OUTREACH

Outreach service is not a new phenomenon for most libraries, but often it does not embrace the full range of programs and services that are part of basic library service. Not infrequently the entire outreach program is regarded as value-added service, for which someone other than the library should pay. With the exception of bookmobile services, outreach services are very often underwritten by grants, either under the Library Services and Construction Act (LSCA) or from a private company or foundation. Sometimes they are the beneficiaries of special fund raising by civic and service clubs. While these are certainly viable ways of funding pilot programs to test outreach services, my view is that outreach services, especially those for children and youth, are *basic and central* to today's library programming if the needs of its community are to be met. Accordingly, these services should be included in the library's regular operating budget.

Public libraries originally—and still most commonly—offered outreach and extension services through their branches and their bookmobile services. A delightful children's book, *Clara and the Bookwagon*, by Nancy Smiler Levinson documents the establishment of "book deposit stations" in churches and general stores in Maryland at the turn of the century. This was a first step toward putting collections in places where people ordinarily congregated. Nevertheless, the Hagerstown head librarian, Mary Lemist Titcomb, realized that there were many people on outlying farms who did not get into town very often. She established a "traveling bookwagon" and regularly traveled the back roads, criss-crossing 500 square miles to bring reading materials out to people. Years ahead of her time, she recognized the responsibility of the library to help people become literate.[2] Many equally creative early outreach programs have been documented in the later nineteenth and early twentieth centuries.

During the 1960s the entire country began to focus seriously on social problems and innovative solutions. It was the time of Lyndon Johnson's "Great Society," Headstart was launched, and war was declared on poverty. Some of our profession's contributions to the social consciousness of the time were documented in *Library Journal*.[3] In New Haven, Connecticut, Meredith Bloss, Director of the New Haven Free Public Library declared that we should use library resources to accomplish great social goals.[4] One element of New Haven's model city antipoverty program was "Story Telling on the Stoops." This program featured itinerant story readers who read to children where they were found—very often on the stoops of the housing developments in the summer.

Another area of outreach that can be documented from the sixties is that of librarians helping those working with disadvantaged youth. In Ohio, Eulalie Steinmetz Ross served as liaison to Headstart, as did Dorothy Perillo and Jean St. Clair in New York at the Queensborough Public Library. Both of these programs included specialized lectures, demonstrations, and practice sessions. Suzanne Glazier writes of Brooklyn Public Library's leading role in extending services outside the library.[5] The rationale of their LSCA-funded program was that bringing services outside the library would avoid cutting off library services for numerous people.

Another innovation came in 1969, when Chicago's Public Library added a social worker to its staff.[6] This recognition of the library-based team's need for a person with specialized training is an important milestone in the delivery of outreach services to diverse populations. Unfortunately, other libraries did not jump to follow this impressive model, and the multidisciplinary approach to meeting communities' needs is yet to be implemented. LSCA federally funded library information and referral programs that emphasized that neighborhood and community tailored services were outreach highlights by the end of the sixties. Then heavy-handed cuts were made in funding just as these pioneer outreach efforts were beginning to be widely replicated. By the early seventies the burgeoning of technology and automation and the lack of adequate funding pushed outreach services into the background. Little information appears in the literature. One wonders if little was done, or if the librarians who were involved in outreach efforts were so overextended that there was no time to record their experiences. With the advent of the national focus on literacy, the importance of early childhood learning, and cultural diversity, model programs began to appear once again. Many of these model programs were funded by private sector sponsors, such as the Bell Atlantic Family Literacy Project in partnership with the Office for Library Outreach Services of the American Library Association.

The American Library Association recognized the importance of outreach services when it established its Office for Library Outreach Services (OLOS) in 1972. This Office has a threefold statement of purpose:

> . . . to promote the provision of library service to the urban and rural poor, of all ages and to those people who are discriminated against because they belong to a minority group . . . to encourage the development of user-oriented informational and educational library services to meet the needs of the urban and rural poor, ethnic minority groups, the underemployed, school dropouts, the semiliterate and illiterate and those isolated by cultural differences . . . and to insure that librarians and others have information, access to technical assistance and continuing education opportunities to assist them in developing effective outreach programs.[7]

That statement of purpose clearly summarizes the broad scope of programs and services that are encompassed by the term *outreach*. Yet, more often than not, outreach services are very difficult to put into action. The two main reasons for this are lack of training in these specialized areas and lack of funds. *Managing Library Outreach Programs* will address both those problems.

VALUE OF OFF-SITE PROGRAMS

The first step toward success is the most important: commitment to the goal of making library services available to all. We need to face reality and understand that not everyone is comfortable within our traditional library boundaries. The buildings are imposing, the amounts of information are overwhelming, unfamiliar cultural manifestations are threatening. In many instances, people don't know that the library has something for them. Outreach services, also known as "the off-site approach," offer librarians the opportunity to open up communication about the library and its services *on the user's own turf.* It gives librarians the chance to observe and listen to the population intended to be served, so that the barriers can be overcome. Bringing the library outside its walls requires a change of perception about the library and its roles, both on the part of the librarians and of the users. We must recognize that society is in a constant state of flux and "we always did it that way" is not a solution, but an evasion of responsibility. This recognition clears the way for the library to function as a critical access point for information and personal development resources, so that it is perceived as a source of personal empowerment for its users.

ENDNOTES

1. Charles McClure, et al., *Planning and Role Setting for Public Libraries* (Chicago: American Library Association, 1987), 37.

2. Nancy Smiler Levinson, *Clara and the Bookwagon* (New York: Harper and Row, 1988).

3. Meredith Bloss, "Take a Giant Step," *Library Journal* 91:2 (Jan. 15, 1966): 324-336.

4. *Ibid.*

5. Suzanne Glazier, "Who's Non-Verbal," *Library Journal*, 91:2 (Jan. 15, 1966): 341-343.

6. ———, "Staff Social Worker Sparks Chicago," *Library Journal*, 93:23 (Dec. 15, 1968): 460-78.

7. "ALA offices: Statement of Purposes," in ALA *Handbook of Organization* (Chicago: American Library Association, Annual).

2 IN SEARCH OF LIBRARY PATRONS

TARGETING THE INDIVIDUAL

All libraries have some segments of population in their service area that are underserved. Outreach service is one of the techniques that librarians can employ to help them reach these populations. The needs of communities vary—no two are exactly alike. Careful assessment of a specific community's needs and planning to meet these needs is essential to a successful outreach program. How to do these assessments will be discussed in more detail later in this chapter. Simply put, the message of outreach services is that there is an adjustment in the delivery of services, not only in sensitivity to the public's need, but also to the public's location. The services must be designed to help people overcome language, cultural, and social barriers. Because all libraries are different, there are some significant national indicators that should be used by local libraries in determining their roles.

These statistical tools, which the local librarian can use as a barometer for local trends, require careful consideration. Demographics provide the library with an overview of potential patrons, detailing their age, sex, race, educational levels, income levels, and ethnic backgrounds. In work with children, the library needs to know family characteristics: what is the size of the family, how many families are headed by single parents? Some specific examples include the rate at which unmarried teenage women are giving birth. In 1989 it was 25 per 1,000 births, up from 5 per 1000 in 1950.[1] There is also a rising number of children under 18 who are living with the one guardian. In 1965 it was it was 10 percent of children; in 1989 it was 22 percent. In minority families the differences are even greater—54 percent of African-American children and 28 percent of Hispanic children are part of a single guardian family.[2] These issues have wide-ranging implications for libraries. Teenage mothers may not complete their education; therefore they may not have the necessary literacy skills to obtain employment, let alone read to their children. Economically, there are also considerations. A parent's inability to secure suitable employment means that the children are going to be disadvantaged in important areas—like not having formal preschool available to them. Another economic indicator to be taken into consideration is the makeup of the work force. In 1960, only 19 percent of mothers who had children under the age of six worked. In 1990, 59 percent of all children under age six had their main caregiver in the work force.[3]

A conclusion to be drawn from this is that there is an increase in attendance at day care centers—a service "outlet" that the library may not have considered. Social conditions within the community play a role in the types of services the library works to develop. The cultural climate, including clubs, religious organizations, and ethnic traditions all need to be assessed as the library is developing strategies to accomplish its mission. Identifying the underserved means recognizing problems these groups face and developing solutions through library service that will enhance their living skills. *America 2000*, the recently developed prescription and goals for America's education system, recognizes that students live and learn in a setting that is larger than the school.[4] Libraries, in a very broad context, are part of the solution, and can use diversified services to help the nation meet these goals.

COMMUNITY NEED ASSESSMENT PROCESS

The Public Library Association's publications, *Planning and Role Setting for Libraries* and *Output Measures for Public Libraries* are two comprehensive manuals that can assist librarians in their community assessment. In addition to identifying the community's unmet needs, the library must examine how it is perceived within the community. *Planning and Role Setting for Public Libraries* gives some very sound advice about the information gathering process. It suggests that the best information will be obtained by a combination of both objective and subjective evaluations.[5]

In order to get a clear picture of the interrelationship of the library and the community, I find the "walk-about," or if you prefer, the "drive-about" method, to be one of the most helpful. Walking or driving around the community gives you the opportunity to define its unique characteristics. You should take stock of various neighborhoods, schools, churches, shopping areas, playgrounds, day care facilities, etc. It is important to repeat this process at different times of the day and on weekends as well as weekdays to give you an accurate picture of the community.

How do you find out what information or help people need that libraries—your library—might provide for them? Bear in mind that people may want to know many things, but they usually—very educated people too—don't think of the library as having the answers.

You can ask by various means: "What would you like to know?—the library has answers." You can do this using a flyer given out in the street by staff, volunteers, or club members—or even put in grocery bags at the market check-out counter. Some attention-grabbers might be: "How do I find out about health care at home?" or "What training would I need to start a small business?" or "How do I work for a high school diploma if I dropped out of school early?"

Ask community opinion leaders—bank officers, reporters, service workers—what questions they get in the course of a month: Health questions? Legal questions? Child care questions? Money questions? Suggest that they send people to the library for answers. When you are in your car listen to the call-in shows on radio to see what people are bothered by or interested in. Sharpen up your own telephone reference services, and keep good records of queries. You find out a lot by listening, and this will help you create the foundation for your outreach programs.

Another important technique is to attend community events. Include members of your family as well as your staff. There is an endless variety of activities from which to choose, and the list in itself is quite telling. Community celebrations, parades, church fairs, concerts, and sports activities all can be used to broaden the scope of your knowledge about people who may be potential patrons. In addition to providing first-hand information, community participation offers greater insights than the more formal survey methods. Informal interviews or casual discussions with people attending these events are a terrific way to find out what they want. At these events people are much more likely to be candid than in a formal interview situation. It also gives people in the community a chance to meet you in an informal setting that shows your interest in them.

For time-saving techniques, we must remember to use many of the existing information resources that have already been compiled. Factual details about communities are compiled by the market research departments of companies and economic or tourist districts. They are often willing to share this data with the library. Local colleges and universities also maintain such data. Local colleges and business schools may even have students willing to do some original research for you as part of their coursework. They gain valuable experience while providing valuable original research for your planning process—a classic "win-win" scenario.

Much data is already available in census documents, city and county directories and data books, state government publications, and even in local telephone books and newspapers. Other reliable sources of data are the local chamber of commerce and local divisions of trade associations. An objective look at the community will help you decide on the extent and the type of outreach services needed in your area. Being objective will also help you overcome the frustration of not being able to give full attention to all needs of all people. Whatever method of community analysis you choose to employ, you will want to keep written records on hand from which to develop your plans. The records you prepare this year will be the baseline for measuring your success, facilitating trend analysis, and documenting a winning case for your next budget proposal.

Worksheets 2-1a and 2-2a will help you gather and organize data about the community. It is important for you to remember that these are *samples*, and thus *general*. They are meant to serve as a starting point to which you may need to add specific qualities or characteristics appropriate to your particular situation. Worksheets 2-1b and 2-2b show the same forms filled out with data from the Meriden Library.

LIBRARY CHARACTERISTICS

Just as you need as much information as possible about the community, you must also have accurate and up-to-date information about all aspects of your library. A complete picture about your library is basic to the execution of any program. While it may seem to be an overwhelming task at first, once the information is gathered it will be used over and over again, and updating it will be relatively quick and easy. Use the checklists in Worksheet 2-3a to develop a profile of your library. Again, Worksheet 2-3b shows the completed profile for the Meriden Library.

ENDNOTES

1. National Center for Education Statistics, *Youth Indicators, 1991*. Washington, DC, 1991, p. 2.

2. Ibid., p. 3.

3. Ibid., p. 4.

4. U. S. Department of Education, *America 2000: An Education Strategy*. Washington, DC, 1991, p. 31.

5. American Library Association, *Handbook of Organization*. Chicago, 1991.

WORKSHEET 2-1a

**COMMUNITY PROFILE CHECKLIST: CHILDREN'S SERVICES
INFORMAL DATA OBSERVATION FORM**

Library Name or Branch:

Neighborhood/District: _____

Person Completing Survey: _____

Date: _____

Event Attended: _____

Process Employed: _____

Facilities	*No. of Units*	*Special Characteristics*
Amusements/Recreation:		
Business Outlets:		
Banks:		
Churches and Synagogues:		
Community/Youth Centers:		
Day Care Centers:		
Elementary Schools - Public:		
Elementary Schools - Private:		
Health Clinics:		
Jr. High School - Public/Private:		
Homeless/Abused women's and children's shelter:		
Legal aid resources:		

(continued)

WORSHEET 2-1b

**COMMUNITY PROFILE CHECKLIST: CHILDREN'S SERVICES
INFORMAL DATA OBSERVATION FORM**

Library Name or Branch	*Meriden Public Library*
Neighborhood/District:	1 Library in town
Person Completing Survey:	M. Trotta
Date:	9-26-92
Event Attended:	Columbus Celebration
Process Employed:	Informal observation and talking with other community individuals.

Facilities	*No. of Units*	*Special Characteristics*
Amusements/Recreation:	15 public parks, 15 playgrounds, golf course, 3 public pools, 30 tennis courts, 25 ball fields	
Business Outlets:	100+	
Banks:	12	
Churches and Synagogues:	26	
Community/Youth Centers:	YMCA + YWCA have programs	
Day Care Centers:	12 businesses - many family centers	
Elementary Schools - Public:	8	
Elementary Schools - Private:	5	
Health Clinics:	2	
Jr. High School - Public/Private:	3/4	
Homeless/Abused women's and children's shelter:		2
Legal aid resources:		3

(continued)

WORKSHEET 2-1a   (Cont.)

**COMMUNITY PROFILE CHECKLIST: CHILDREN'S SERVICES
INFORMAL DATA OBSERVATION FORM**

Facilities	*No. of Units*	*Special Characteristics*
Nursery Schools:		
Playgrounds:		
Restaurants:		
Shopping Areas:		
Other:		

Other Factors:

Civic Groups:

Economic Overview:

Ethnic Background:

Religious Organizations:

Social Clubs:

Other:

Personal Contacts Made:

Name	Address
Affiliation	Phone No.
Comments	

(continued)

WORKSHEET 2-1b   (Cont.)

COMMUNITY PROFILE CHECKLIST: CHILDREN'S SERVICES INFORMAL DATA OBSERVATION FORM

Facilities	*No. of Units*	*Special Characteristics*
Nursery Schools:	5	
Playgrounds:	15	
Restaurants:	100+	
Shopping Areas:	3 Key areas, 1 bordering Wallingford	
Other:		

Other Factors:

Civic Groups:	All major clubs including Lions, Jaycees, Kiwanis, Rotary.
Economic Overview:	Distressed—6.8% unemployment.
Ethnic Background:	Mixed—large population of second generation European immigrants, 22% Hispanic, 7% Black.
Religious Organizations:	Several associated with churches.
Social Clubs:	Elks, Eagles, Masons, and many church related.
Other:	Community Action, political committees.

Personal Contacts Made:

Name	Address
Affiliation	Phone No.
Comments	

D. Cooper   123 Main Street   Newspaper   634-1234   Celebration related

A. Olds   456 Elm Street   Council   237-5678   General comments

WORKSHEET 2-2a

COMMUNITY PROFILE CHECKLIST: CHILDREN'S SERVICES FORMAL DATA COLLECTION

*Library Name:*_____

Date:_____

Person Completing Survey: _____

Sources Consulted to Compile Data:

General Information:

Total Town Population: _____

Total Child Population: _____

    % of Child Population to Total: _____

        Age Ranges: _____

            0 to 4 years: _____

            5 to 9 years: _____

            10 to 14 years: _____

Per capita income: _____

Unemployment rate:_____

Percentage of population over 25 with:

  High School Degree: _____

  College Degree: _____

Registered library users: _____

Actual borrowers: _____   (continued)

WORSHEET 2-2b

COMMUNITY PROFILE CHECKLIST: CHILDREN'S SERVICES FORMAL DATA COLLECTION

Library Name:	*Meriden Public*
Date:	10/13/92
Person Completing Survey:	M. Trotta
Sources Consulted to Compile Data:	1990 Census, City Government Files, Board of Education Data, Comprehensive Housing Affordability Strategy

General Information:

Total Town Population:	59,419
Total Child Population:	14,051 (to age 18)
% of Child Population to Total:	23.4%

Age Ranges:

0 to 4 years:	4,530
5 to 9 years:	2,613
10 to 14 years:	4,350

Per capita income: $15,618

Unemployment rate: 6.8%

Percentage of population over 25 with:

High School Degree: 72.6%

College Degree: 15.8%

Registered library users: 59%

Actual borrowers: 52%

(continued)

WORKSHEET 2-2a   (Cont.)

**COMMUNITY PROFILE CHECKLIST: CHILDREN'S SERVICES
FORMAL DATA COLLECTION**

Information on Families and Households:

Total number of families: _____

Median family income: _____

Percentage of children/youth in single parent families: _____

Percentage of two-income families: _____

Percentage of families below poverty line:_____

List racial/ethnic/language groups:_____

Information About The Community:

Number of Day Care Centers: _____

Number of Home Day Care Providers:_____

Number of children under 5 in day care: _____

Number of children 5 to 9 years in day care: _____

Number of Nursery Schools: _____

Number of children attending nursery schools: _____

Number of public schools:

      Elementary: _____

      Junior High: _____

Number of children enrolled in public schools:

      Elementary: _____

      Junior High: _____

(continued)

WORKSHEET 2-2b   (Cont.)

**COMMUNITY PROFILE CHECKLIST: CHILDREN'S SERVICES
FORMAL DATA COLLECTION**

Information on Families and Households:

Total number of families: 15,809

Median family income: 36,211

Percentage of children/youth in single parent families: 28%

Percentage of two-income families: 67%

Percentage of families below poverty line: 6.3%

List racial/ethnic/language groups: Spanish, French, Polish, Italian, Vietnamese, Indian, Portuguese, Pakistani.

Information About The Community:

Number of Day Care Centers: 12

Number of Home Day Care Providers: 30

Number of children under 5 in day care: 605

Number of children 5 to 9 years in day care: 200

Number of Nursery Schools: 5

Number of children attending nursery schools: 1,284

Number of public schools:

     Elementary: 8

     Junior High: 2

Number of children enrolled in public schools:

     Elementary: 4,700

     Junior High: 1,600

(continued)

WORKSHEET 2-2a   (Cont.)

**COMMUNITY PROFILE CHECKLIST: CHILDREN'S SERVICES
FORMAL DATA COLLECTION**

Number of private schools:

Elementary: _____

Junior High: _____

Number of children enrolled in private schools:

Elementary: _____

Junior High: _____

Newspapers: _____

Radio and T.V. Stations: _____

Other: (Museums, hospitals, amusements, etc.)

Information services other than the library (describe):

Clubs and Organizations that have interests in children:

Club Name _____ Address _____

Phone # _____ Contact Person _____

Trends in the Community:

List *all* that you can think of (They may not seem relevant at the time, but they have a way of helping you when you least expect it). You may also want to collect items from newspapers, etc. and clip them into your survey, for future use.

WORKSHEET 2-2b   (Cont.)

**COMMUNITY PROFILE CHECKLIST: CHILDREN'S SERVICES
FORMAL DATA COLLECTION**

Number of private schools:

Elementary: 8

Junior High: 2

Number of children enrolled in private schools:

Elementary: 1,200

Junior High: 300

Newspapers: 1

Radio and T.V. Stations: 1

Other: (Museums, hospitals, amusements, etc.) 1 hospital, 1 historical society, 1 pending museum.

Information services other than the library (describe): Infoline, Trade board, Tourism Commission.

Clubs and Organizations that have interests in children:

Club Name	Address	Phone #	Contact Person
Junior Womans	62 Oak Street	235-1909	S. Frey
Fire Fighter's Aux.	116 Lincoln Ave.	237-6543	A. Ray

Trends in the Community:

Community under redevelopment for downtown area—possibility of alliances. Overall, trying to rebuild image, economics, etc.—how can we be of help? Meriden is a town of approximately 60,000 people, located in Central Connecticut. Once a booming industrial center, the town has been struggling economicly during the past decade. Efforts are being made to rebuild the town, and to attract new businesses into the area. Most of Meriden's population work outside the town. In many ways, the town mirrors the social and economic distress of some other Connecticut cities— New Britain and Waterbury. The housing is expensive and the unemployment rate is 1% above the state's average. Although it is fairly small, the community has a very diverse ethnic backbone.

WORKSHEET 2-3a

LIBRARY PROFILE CHECKLIST

Collection Information:	*Print*	*Nonprint*
Total number of pieces of material in library:		
Total number of children's materials in library:		
Percentage of children's to the total collection:		
Most recent annual number of adult items purchased:		
Most recent annual number of children's items purchased:		
Most recent annual number of adult items weeded:		
Most recent annual number of children's items weeded:		
Total library circulation:		
Total circulation of children's materials:		
Percentage of children's circulation to total:		
Total Registered Borrowers:		
Total Registered Child Borrowers:		
Percentage of Child Borrowers to the Total Population:		

(continued)

WORKSHEET 2-3b

LIBRARY PROFILE CHECKLIST

Collection Information:	*Print*	*Nonprint*
Total number of pieces of material in library:	180,000	6,000
Total number of children's materials in library:	60,000	2,000
Percentage of children's to the total collection:	33%	
Most recent annual number of adult items purchased:	6,000	
Most recent annual number of children's items purchased:	2,000	
Most recent annual number of adult items weeded:	500	
Most recent annual number of children's items weeded:	200	
Total library circulation:	260,000	
Total circulation of children's materials:	85,000	
Percentage of children's circulation to total:	33%	
Total Registered Borrowers:	35,600	
Total Registered Child Borrowers:	11,748	
Percentage of Child Borrowers to the Total Population:	33%	

(continued)

WORKSHEET 2-3a   (Cont.)

LIBRARY PROFILE CHECKLIST

Staffing Information:

	Total	*Full-Time*	*Part-Time*
Total number of employees:			
Total number of professional:			
Total number of support staff:			
Total number of volunteers:			

    adult
    children
    young adult

Financial Resources

Total Operating Budget:

Expenditure per capita:

Total materials budget:	*Print*	*Nonprint*
adult		
children		
young adult		

Total program budget:
    adult
    children's
    young adult

Facilities:

Square footage of Library:

Square footage of Children's Department:

Square footage of Young Adult area:

Number of service outlets:

Total hours of service per week at all outlets:

(continued)

WORKSHEET 2-3b   (Cont.)

LIBRARY PROFILE CHECKLIST

Staffing Information:

	Total	Full-Time	Part-Time
Total number of employees:	43	20	23
Total number of professional:	14	10	4
Total number of support staff:	29	10	19
Total number of volunteers:	85		

adult	75
children	6
young adult	4

Financial Resources:

Total Operating Budget:	$1,200,000.00
Expenditure per capita:	$20/per cap.

Total materials budget:	*Print*	*Nonprint*
adult	138,000	5,000
children	25,000	2,000
young adult	2,000	0

Total program budget:

adult	4,000
children's	2,700
young adult	300

Facilities:

Square footage of Library:	52,000
Square footage of Children's Department:	12,000
Square footage of Young Adult area:	600
Number of service outlets:	1
Total hours of service per week at all outlets:	59 hrs.

(continued)

WORKSHEET 2-3a   (Cont.)

Facilities:

Total hours of children's service hours at all outlets:

Total hours of young adult service hours at all outlets:

Percentage of children's hours to total:

Percentage of young adult hours to total:

Total seating capacity at all service outlets:

Total seating capacity in Children's Department:

Total seating capacity in Young Adult Department:

Other features (parking, accessibility, etc.):

Programs:	*Adult*	*Children*	*Y/A*
Average number of in-house programs per week:			
Average number of outreach programs per week:			
Average program attendance per week:			
Other:			

WORKSHEET 2-3b   (Cont.)

Facilities:

Total hours of children's service hours at all outlets:	59 hrs
Total hours of young adult service hours at all outlets:	58 hrs
Percentage of children's hours to total:	100%
Percentage of young adult hours to total:	100%
Total seating capacity at all service outlets:	300
Total seating capacity in Children's Department:	100
Total seating capacity in Young Adult Department:	50
Other features (parking, accessibility, etc.):	Adjacent lot and totally accessible

Programs:	*Adult*	*Children*	*Y/A*
Average number of in-house programs per week:	3	12	6 per yr
Average number of outreach programs per week:	1/mo	2	--
Average program attendance per week:	70	150	15
Other:			

3 COALITIONS AND ALLIES

PARTNERSHIPS THAT MAKE A DIFFERENCE

After you have identified who is "out there" in your community and believe you know something of what their needs might be, the next crucial step in developing outreach services is to identify "kindred spirits"—other individuals, groups, or agencies with a service philosophy that is similar to your own. They are the ones who can help you develop as well as implement the services that are necessary in your community. These alliances that you build will serve to extend the library's capability of reaching out in many different ways. Some alliances will lead to the provision of an off-site location to which you can bring your services; others will provide you with the personal contacts you may need to reach targeted groups; still others will support you with in-kind donations and the other financial support that often is the key to your program's success. Simply speaking, alliances are really strategic resources that enable you to adjust the type of service, its delivery, and its location to meet the needs of your targeted clientele. One of the often overlooked yet important rules about alliances is that they should benefit all the participants.

Get started by thinking about some benefits that the library can offer future partners. They might be as simple as routine services that are not widely known: providing free meeting space; putting together subject bibliographies or collections; having a library staff member become a board member for an agency; arranging publicity so that a donation to the program receives community recognition. Each agency or organization has a mission for being, just as the library does. The benefit that is most often sought by potential participants is one that will help them accomplish their mission. Receiving some support from the library will make them more eager to assist you in reaching your goal of providing outreach services.

The other prerequisite for smooth cooperative efforts is to have clearly defined roles and responsibilities for all parties. Each organization involved must understand the other's mission as well as the purpose of forming a coalition or alliance. Strategic plans, budget requirements, and relationship policies must be established with input from all the concerned parties. Ways to deal with disagreements and partners not meeting obligations must also be clearly established and understood. In some cases, agencies or organizations may find that some reorganization is necessary before they can participate in a coalition. In all cases, flexibility and a willingness to compromise are required to make these alliances fully functional. There's no argument that these coalitions do take a great deal of nurturing! But, it is truly worth the effort, and the benefits to your library will become obvious.

Alliances and coalitions are extremely valuable to the library because the participants possess important assets, expert knowledge, and a diversity of potential that the library just does not have on its own. In order to get coalitions to work, the library staff will have to be aggressive, assertive, and dedicated to creating a shift in people's perspectives about the library and its services. Simultaneously, there is a need to keep a clear picture in our mind about our partners and what role the alliance will have to help them meet their mission in the community.

THREE GOOD SOURCES

There are some subtle differences involved in forming different kinds of alliances depending on the needs of the other partners. Three promising areas that the library should investigate are: social service agencies; civic clubs and other service organizations; and local businesses and foundations. While your "umbrella" reason for forming these partnerships is to improve outreach services, the specific reason why you form an alliance may vary. Therefore, it is appropriate to consider some variables.

Social Service Agencies

Agencies are the most logical place to start because there are so many that provide services to children and their parents. These groups already have our target group as clients, and a clear benefit of working with them would be to have access to this audience. Also, like the library, they are nonprofits.

The list of resources at the end of this book includes several national organizations that serve parents and children. Contact them to find their local affiliates. One of the most useful tools that you have at your disposal is the phone book! It will enable you to locate public and private agencies within your town and state. This list should include child welfare agencies, churches and synagogues, day care centers, family-based caregivers, literacy volunteers, homeless shelters, clinics, child and youth services, health and human resources agencies, schools, parks, and recreation departments, pediatricians, dentists, and related health offices, as a start. You may find that there are already some networks among these groups, and they are usually amazed to think that the library would be interested in joining them! The library's over-arching goal is really the same as theirs: to improve the quality of life for people. Our approach is a little different from theirs and library services could offer them new strategies for meeting their goals. For best results, you should call and set up an appointment to meet with the director or a senior staff member. Begin to identify the ways that you may work together to develop services that are appropriate for the clients that particular agency serves. Worksheet 3-1a outlines some key questions that you should address with each of these agencies. Worksheet 3-1b includes data from a typical social service agency.

It is not always possible to complete the worksheet on your first visit, but it is an accurate and effective way of compiling information that will be useful to both agencies. Remember that alliances are *partnerships* and you should give the agency a copy of your worksheet as well as information about the library.

Civic Clubs and Service Organizations

These organizations usually have been "bettering" the community as part of their overall purpose for existing. Your local Chamber of Commerce will have a list of organizations and local newspapers are a key source of information about them as well. Sometimes the clubs are local chapters of state or national organizations that have sponsored events nationwide. Others may set service goals based on community needs, and they may undertake fundraising projects as well as providing volunteers. Some examples are the American Association of University Women, the Kiwanis, the Key Clubs, Rotary, Lions, and Jaycees.

Interview a leader from the organization to acquire specific data about the club. Use Worksheets 3-2a and 3-2b to organize your data. Call first to set up an appointment with the individual in charge. Keep their needs in mind: will someone from the library join their group? Will someone serve on the board? Very often, with teen groups especially, the library will be asked to log the volunteer hours served, and to write recommendations. Be prepared!

Local Business, Foundations, and Private Partners

There are many other organizations that can be called upon to play an important role in your outreach program. Local busi-

WORKSHEET 3-1a

SOCIAL SERVICES PARTNER IDENTIFICATION WORKSHEET

Librarian: _____

Date: _____

Agency name: Contact person: Chief Executive:

Agency address: Phone number:

Agency's mission:

Number of people agency serves:

      Children: _____

      Adults: _____

      Youth: _____

Funding Source/Auspices: _____

Services agency offers clients:

Days of week/time services available:

Ways library could participate in already existing services:

New programs that the library can develop with the agency:

Other:

Cost of program to library: $_____

Cost of program to agency: $_____

Other possible partners:

WORKSHEET 3-1b

SOCIAL SERVICES PARTNER IDENTIFICATION WORKSHEET

Librarian: Lyn Jones

Date: 8-20-92

Agency name: Chrysalis   Contact person: Chief Executive:

Anne King   Anne King

Agency address: P.O. Box 123   Phone number: 630-4357

Agency's mission: A shelter for battered women.

Number of people agency serves (yearly):   Children: 100+

Adults: 50-75

Youth: 25

Funding Source/Auspices: United Way and private contributions

Services agency offers clients: Protective shelter, food,
clothing, until parents are
able to re-establish themselves.

Days of week/time services available: 24/day, daily, all year.

Ways library could participate in already existing services:
Offer story programs.
Offer book collections.
Support agency's information and referral services.

New programs that the library can develop with the agency:
Work with adults to give them information on developing career skills, job resources.
Other:

Cost of program to library: 1 Story hr/wk @ $15 = $480.00

Cost of program to agency: $ 20 (misc.)

Other possible partners: Literacy Volunteers, Y.W.C.A.

WORKSHEET 3-2a

CIVIC CLUB/SERVICE CLUB PARTNER IDENTIFICATION WORKSHEET

Librarian:

Date:

Club Name: **Club Contact:**

Address: **Phone No:**

Club Purpose:

Number of People in Club:

Activities Conducted by Club: **When Held:**

Target Audience of Activities:

Special Interests/Priorities of Club:

Ways Library can Participate in already existing activities:

Ways the Library can develop new activities /programs with the club:

Ways the Library can assist the club with its purpose:

Benefits to the club:

Cost of program to the Library: $_____

Cost of program to the club: $_____

Other possible partners:

WORKSHEET 3-2b

SAMPLE WORKSHEET: CIVIC CLUB/SERVICE CLUB PARTNER INFORMATION

Librarian: Marie Lynd

Date: March 1, 1992.

Club Name: Help Club; **Contact:** Jackie Lee

Address: 101 Main Street **Phone:** 630-HELP

Club Purpose: To provide an organized resource of teen volunteers to help with community events.

Number of People in Club: 42

Activities Conducted by Club: Annual Tag Sale, Kid's Fair, assist at town days.

Target Audience: A nonprofit group that needs volunteers.

Special Interest: Children, senior citizens.

Ways Library Can Participate in Already Existing Activities: Do story hour or other program at Kid's Fair.

Ways the Library Can Develop New Activities/Programs: Sponsor kid/senior test, intergenerational reading programs. Train teens to volunteer to read to kids at various off-site community locations. Club may develop fundraiser to give library additional books it may need.

Ways the Library Can Assist Club with its' Purpose: Provide a variety of volunteer opportunities for club members.

(continued)

WORKSHEET 3-2b   (Cont.)

Benefits to the Club:

      1. Club can arrange to meet in library meeting room at no charge.

      2. Club can put up a display to attract new members in the area.

      3. Librarians who work with the club members can be used by members as references for job or college applications.

Cost of Program to the Library: Proportion of the staff member's salary based on number of hours/week he or she would work with group: *Estimate 2hrs/week @ $15/hr = $30/week.*

Cost of Program to Club: Flyers printing cost, approximately $50. These would communicate what club is doing with the library display materials.

Other Possible Partners: Local printers who might sponsor flyers free of charge; other underwriters to sponsor the fundraising costs so more money can be applied towards books; perhaps a local garage could donate space, water, soap, sponges, and wax for a "car wash." Would the local paper donate ad space?

nesses are often interested in giving something back to the community. Some businesses may have foundations which direct their charitable donations. Private individuals, too, often will donate to specific projects. The steps that we have been through so far will help you set the stage to call upon these groups to assist the library with volunteers, outright cash donations, and in-kind donations.

Your public relations program is really the mechanism for initiating and then establishing these private partnerships. Often these groups will decide whether or not to work with you based on your past performance. Therefore, the sense that you have of the community (who's there and what do they do), and the sense that you have about the library and how it is perceived within this community are of utmost importance. Private sector partners are more likely to endorse programs that they perceive to have common sense—strategic plans that clearly indicate what it is that you are trying to do and how you are planning to achieve it. They will want to know what it is that you will be doing for them and for *their* image in the community.

Developing partnerships with corporations and private citizens is a little different from the methods suggested for social agencies and civic clubs. Even though your purpose in going to them is the same, the twist is that they will be wanting to *interview* you (this is another reason for completing Worksheet 2-3: Library Profile Checklist). So before you put yourself in that position, find out as much as possible about them *before* you approach them for assistance.

Community history is one element of the information you will need. Which individuals are known in the community for their generosity? Why? Is it attached to some specific cause? Are they library users? Are they members of the Friends of the Library? Your local newspaper is an important source. You should read it daily, or as often as it comes out, and keep a card file of potential donors with the information that you glean. Contact these individuals as you need support. Phone contact, if possible, is the best method, followed quickly by a confirming letter.

Information about businesses and foundations is reported in local papers too. Regularly clipping and filing this data makes it available when you need it. A thorough investigation of sources such as the *Foundation Directory* or your statewide foundation directory is advisable if you are approaching organizations for dollars, rather than volunteers or in-kind services. These sources will tell you the amount of money foundations have given in the

WORKSHEET 3-3a

PRIVATE PARTNER INFORMATION

Name:

Address:

Phone:

Giving History:

Special Interests:

Information Sources/Contacts:

Kind of Business: Retail: _____

                              Manufacturing:_____

                              Services: _____

Names of Principals or Owners/Managers:_____

Personal Interests/Concerns of Owners:_____

(Collector or hobbyist; aged parent or handicapped child, etc.)

WORKSHEET 3-3b

PRIVATE PARTNER INFORMATION

Name: United Manufacturing

Address: 332 Lincoln Avenue

Phone: 634-8648

Giving History: Foundation, grants to local institutions: $250-1,500 range.

Special Interests: Education, museums, culture.

Information Sources/Contacts:

Kind of Business: Retail: _____

Manufacturing: nuts, bolts, small hardware

Services: _____

Names of Principals or Owners/Managers: John E. Toon

Personal Interests/Concerns of Owners: Literacy: chairs Children's Fair

past, and the types of organizations they support. Special areas of interest are also listed. You should also make sure you know what the company product is, how long they have been in the area, and other pertinent facts.

Do your homework before approaching a business or foundations. Use Worksheets 3-3 through 3-6 to organize your research. Don't hesitate to form partnerships. Coalitions and alliances do take considerable effort, but the results are very rewarding for all parties involved. Most important of all, they carry the message that the library does recognize that there are problems of all dimensions in every community, and that—together with its partners—it can offer some solutions to these problems.

WORSHEET 3-4

PROPOSAL GROUNDWORK

I. Know *What* you need:

   A. Volunteers:

      1. How many hours a week?

      2. What will they do?

      3. Who will train them?

      4. What are long-term and short-term needs?

      5. What recognition will they receive?

   B. In-Kind Services or Donation:

      1. An amount of the product they make.

      2. A cents-off coupon for their product or service for you to give as an incentive.

      3. Printing services:
         a. Flyers
         b. Bookmarks, etc.

      4. Use of their facility
         a. Meeting room
         b. Outdoor area
         c. When, how long
         d. For what purpose
         e. Liability insurance

   C. Cash Donations:

      1. How much?

      2. What will dollars be used for?
         a. Project outline
         b. Have a budget plan

      3. What percentage of budget are you asking from them?

(continued)

WORKSHEET 3-4 (Cont.)

4. Who else is giving money? They may be concerned if it is a competitor and may be urged to give if they know others have.

5. How is the library supporting this?
    a. You should itemize staff hours and multiply by salary to indicate this match.
    b. You should itemize dollar value of all materials and equipment and supplies you will be using as a match. If you show that *you* gave before you asked for support, your commitment is emphasized.

6. Be specific with your request. Tell them what their dollars will fund.

II. Tell them what recognition they can expect:

A. Photo in newspaper

B. Press story

C. Company name attached to program; i.e., sponsored by: . . . .

D. Other ideas!

III. Remember to say *thank you* publicly and privately:

A. To the company's leadership

B. To *all* individuals in their group who assisted you in your efforts. Remember success really happens when people are connected to people.

IV. Be Prepared:

A. Most companies will expect you to have a written proposal. While the thought of a proposal is overwhelming to many, it really does evolve naturally from the planning process. It does not need to be long, but it must be readable and understandable to someone outside the library, and it should be flexible and offer alternatives.

B. It is a good idea to prepare a proposal for a long term or expensive project in phases. Phase I will accomplish so much and cost so much; Phase II will build on the first, accomplish so much more, and cost . . . . The donor may then elect to fund only Phase I for a start with no guarantee of more funds if the first part is not satisfactory.

WORKSHEET 3-5

PROPOSAL WORKSHEET

Library Name:

Library Mission:

Recent Accomplishments:

Project Name:

Description of the Project: (Be sure to include these items in your description).

Why: Why is the library undertaking this project (goal).

What are the *needs* in this area?

What are the *current efforts* in this area?

What *unique contribution* will your project make or offer?

How: What methods or strategies will you use in your project to achieve it's objective. Present a clear, logical progression of steps and how each component relates to others.

Who: You should clearly demonstrate that your project is "do-able." Specify the roles and the responsibilities of the individuals who will actually be involved in implementing the project.

When: Develop a timetable. It will provide some perspective for those approached and it will help move things along.

What you Need:

How Much? Develop a budget with as much specific information as possible. Remember a budget describes *both* income and *expenses*.

Evaluation and Accountability: Indicate the steps of evaluation the project will have and how the library will account for the time/dollars, etc. that it receives.

This proposal should be sent with a cover-letter to the individual in charge of the company's giving. If you have not been able to determine the name from your research, it is worth a phone call to the company to find this out. If you neglect to do this small detail, your proposal may end up sitting on the wrong person's desk gathering dust!

WORKSHEET 3-6

COVER LETTER CONTENTS

1. Proper salutation.

2. The point of the letter i.e., you are submitting a proposal for their consideration.

3. Explain any special circumstances that are background for the proposal.

4. Express enthusiasm for the proposal.

5. Offer to arrange a meeting—at the library or at a location of their choice—to discuss the proposal.

6. Offer to answer any questions that may arise, and include your phone number, business hours, and position.

7. State that you will be in touch by phone within a given period (two weeks usually works well) to make arrangements to discuss the proposal.

8. Remember to close with a thank you for their time, consideration, etc.

4 HERE, THERE, EVERYWHERE

Off-site programs very often must go beyond the traditional offerings of a public library in order to be effective. The programs that you offer will result from careful consideration of both the community needs *and* the community resources that you have available to you. You should not limit your planning to potential programs that seem easy. Think big. It may take a while to develop the partnerships necessary to an ambitious program, but if there is truly a need, experience has taught me that persistence works. Organizations that work with children are always looking for ways to improve their welfare. At the outset you may run up against some skepticism, but I have found that nothing convinces people like success. Start out with a small, manageable project and document it thoroughly with reports, testimonials, photographs and/or videos. This will become your key that opens doors to cooperation and funding.

This chapter documents some actual programs that were developed to meet the needs of a particular community. As you read through them, you will develop a better understanding of the background work that is recommended in Chapters 2 and 3. A word of caution is necessary here: these models are not intended to be used "as is" in other communities. You may need to do some different programs to operate successfully in your area. You should try out ideas on a limited basis—and don't be afraid to fail. You can always correct and change programs to make them work effectively. Remember that it is difficult, if not impossible, to evaluate realistically if you do not have a clear idea of what you are trying to accomplish. Write down the goals for each project and objectives—and measurable milestones—leading to each goal. Goals and objectives can be adjusted as you get underway.

The following program models are based on a process that begins with a planning stage. There is a lot of brainstorming with partners. Some ideas are accepted, and when tried are successful. Others don't work, so they are eventually abandoned. The implementation process is carefully developed in terms of goals and objectives. The implementation plan, like the goals and objectives themselves, is subject to change if that will make the project work more effectively. Everything is always evaluated and the feedback is used to develop new programs as well as to improve continuing programs. Let us, for example, look at the goals we set for the Doctor's Office Collections, one of our longest running and most satisfactory programs. Our goals are:

- To entertain the children and help parents in a situation that might otherwise be boring or frightening.
- To demonstrate that books can and should be everywhere and that the library is a part of your everyday life.
- To build awareness of the integration of the library into the solutions of community needs.
- To introduce books and the library's riches and invite follow up visits.

Related objectives might be:

- To involve at least half of the doctors'/dentists' offices and health care clinics in the community and get favorable comments from some of them.
- To involve in the program, as volunteers, at least ten members of an influential community organization—in this case the American Association of University Women (AAUW)—which can take pride in making the program a success.
- To see at least three families a month who either come to the library for the first time or comment favorably on the DOC project when they come in.

DOCTOR'S OFFICE COLLECTION

Program Purpose: To broaden children's exposure to quality children's books.

Program Background: The Doctor's Office Collection Program (affectionately labeled DOC) is intended to provide pleasurable reading materials to children while they are waiting to be seen by the doctor. Children's librarians believe that exposing children to good books can turn an apprehensive wait into a pleasurable reading experience, which in turn encourages literacy. The program is also an innovative way to introduce library services to families. The goal is to place small collections (5 to 10 books) in the offices of pediatricians, family practitioners, dentists, and health clinics throughout the community (see Figures 4-1 and 4-2).

Materials Required: We recommend using hardbound, trade picture books. *Curious George*, and *Make Way for Ducklings* are popular titles. (*See* page 50 for a list of suggestions.) The number needed will vary depending on the number of offices that will be served, and the size of the collections. Hardbound books are recommended because of their durability, their aesthetic value, and greater recognition value that these are indeed *library* books. Other materials needed include bags or boxes to carry and display the materials, promotional materials, and standard library processing supplies. Over time, we have found it more efficient to have a duplicate set of books so that we can drop off a new set and bring the old set of books back to the library for repair.

IMPLEMENTATION STEPS

1. Determine the health care facilities in the community that would be appropriate locations.
2. Call their offices and explain the services (see attached script).
3. Decide on the collection size for each location.
4. Secure funding. (Funding might be found within the library's budget from LSCA grants, grants from local foundations or from a civic volunteer group. If so, it is a nice touch to include a bookplate, "Gift of the xyz Club" in each title for further recognition.)
5. Identify a community group whose members would regularly deliver the materials to selected locations.
6. Select and order the books.
7. Process the books. To promote the library, they should have the library's name a letter from the librarian, and some identifying symbol (see Figure 4-2).
8. Develop a circulation procedure—the simpler the better! We use author entries and copy numbers on standard book cards. To circulate, we pull the book cards and keep them with a "library card" for each of the locations.

Figure 4-1 Sample Letter to Participating Doctors

Main Street Public Library
105 Main Street, Anytown, Connecticut 06450
Phone: (203) 233-READ

Dear Dr._____:

The Main Street Public Library, in conjunction with the Anytown Chapter of the American Association of University Women (AAUW) is initiating a new program for library outreach.

Doctor's Office Collection (DOC) is designed to bring books to children who are waiting to be seen by doctors and dentists. During the waiting period, children may be apprehensive, as well as tired or bored. We feel that their wait will be brightened by the availability of appealing picture books, and their minds challenged by exposure to pleasurable reading materials.

AAUW volunteers will place small collections in waiting rooms of the participating doctors and dentists. The doctor and his staff are not responsible for maintaining the collection beyond reasonable care. The books are clearly marked with the Main Street Public Library ownership. They also carry the "DOC" seal which identifies them as a part of this project, and a letter to parents about available library services. AAUW members will replace the collection every six weeks with a fresh assortment.

We are pleased that your office will be participating in this project. We feel that is an important part of developing literacy skills early in life. If you have questions about this service, or about any of the services offered by the Library, please contact me.

Thank you so much for your help!

Sincerely,

Marcia Trotta
Director of Children's Services

> ### Figure 4-2 A Letter to Parents is Glued in Each Book
>
> **Main Street Public Library**
> **105 Main Street, Anytown, Connecticut 06450**
> **Phone: (203) 238-2344**
>
> Dear Parents,
>
> The Doctor's Office Collection (DOC) is designed to provide your children with pleasurable reading materials while they wait for the doctor to see them.
>
> These books are from the Children's Library at the Main Street Public Library and are thoughtfully brought to the Doctor's office by volunteers from the American Association of University Women (AAUW).
>
> We hope that you and your children enjoy this service and we invite you to visit the Main Street Public Library and make use of our many other services.
>
> Hope to see you soon,
>
>
> Marcia Trotta
> Director of Children's Services

9. Develop any other promotional materials that you would like delivered, and add to the collections. This could be bibliographies, the library's calendar, program flyers, etc.

10. Arrange a schedule for volunteers' pick up and delivery. We found that changing the collections every four to six weeks was best. So that volunteers need make only one trip to each site, we ask them to pick up the fresh collections at the library first, deliver them to the offices and pick up the collection there at the same time, and then return all the used collections to the library for repair.

11. Send a thank-you note to the doctor's office staff for their assistance.

12. Send a thank-you to the volunteers for their efforts. If this service is done by a civic group or club, write an

article for their newsletter. You might also want to write a commendation to a state or national group if they are so affiliated.

13. Send a press release to the local paper and other media about the program.

14. Evaluate the program regularly. This process should include the volunteers, follow-up with the location sites, and feedback from patrons.

HINTS FOR A SUCCESSFUL PROGRAM

1. Change the collections regularly.

2. Expect that some books will get heavy use and will not last as long as other circulating books. To cope with this, have enough extra copies of materials on hand.

3. Make clear everyone's responsibility in the program:

   Doctor's offices: Provide the display space and reasonable care for materials. They are not responsible for lost or damaged materials.

   Volunteers: They are to pick up materials at the library on a mutually agreed upon date, deliver the materials to the locations, pick up and return the used collections to the library.

   Library: Coordination of the project, selection and processing of books, and promotion.

4. Remember to say *thank you* to everyone involved in making this service work.

SAMPLE SCRIPT: CALLS TO DOCTOR'S OFFICES

Ask for office manager. If none, they will indicate to whom you should speak.

"Hello my name is _____. I am the children's librarian at the _____ public library. Do you have a few minutes to discuss a service that our library offers?" *(If the answer is yes, continue on. If no, ask when it would be convenient to call back, then go on from here.)*

"We offer an outreach program to doctor's offices. A volunteer will drop off a small collection of children's books for your waiting room once a month. There is no charge for this service, nor is there one for missing books. Our goal is to have the children exposed to library materials while they wait for your services. Each of the books will have our address and phone number so that they can contact us with any questions. Would your office be interested in such a service?" *(Everyone has always said yes!)*

"That's great. The volunteer who will drop off your collection is _____, from _____. (He or she) will be in during your regular office hours, if that is convenient. Again, we will send you a letter of confirmation. My name is _____; please call me if I can be of any help to you. Thank you and goodbye."

SAMPLE BUDGET

Doctor's Office Collection (Based on 100 books):

Materials	Books:	$800.00
	Processing Supplies:	100.00
	Cartons, Bags:	40.00
	Postage:	10.00
Staffing	*20 Hours @ $15 /hour*	*300.00*
	Total	**$1,250.00**

Volunteer staff requires no direct cash outlay. An annual luncheon, however, or some similar event should be considered as recognition of their services and could perhaps be underwritten by an interested organization or individual.

Figure 4-3 Book Distribution Information Form

Location:

Contact Person: Phone:_____

Ages of Children: Number of Children:_____

Special Interests:

Information taken by: Date:_____

SOME SUGGESTED DOC TITLES

Criteria for Selections: Quality picture books, trade editions, which offer pure entertainment. We do not think it is appropriate to have books on going to the dentist, or doctor, or books that deal with various ailments, in this collection. The purpose is to expose children to the enjoyment of reading rather than to provide "bibliotherapy." There are, of course, numerous other selections that would be appropriate choices for this project, and many other lists that you could use to help you make choices that would work in your program, but the following have worked well in Meriden:

Ackerman, Karen. *Song and Dance Man*. Knopf, 1988.

Alexander, Martha. *Boho's Dream*. Dial Press, 1970.

Anglund, Joan Walsh. *In a Pumpkin Shell*. Harcort, Brace, 1960.

Bang, Molly. *The Paper Crane*. Greenwillow, 1985.

Bright, Robert. *Georgie and the Noisy Ghost*. Doubleday, 1971.

Burningham, John. *Seasons*. Bobbs-Merrill, 1968.

Cleary, Beverly. *Janet's Thingamajigs*. Morrow, 1987.

Cohen, Miriam. *See You in Second Grade!* Greenwillow, 1989.

De Paola, Tomie. *Andy (That's My Name)*. Prentice-Hall, 1973.

De Paola, Tomie. *The Art Lesson*. Putnam, 1989.

Fatio, Louise. *Happy Lion*. McGraw, 1954.

Flack, Marjorie. *Ask Mr. Bear*. Macmillan, 1932.

Goldone, Paul. *Three Bears*. Scholastic Book Services, 1972.

Hayes, Sarah. *Eat Up, Gemma*. Lothrop, 1988.

Hutchins, Pat. *Goodnight Owl*. E. M. Hale, 1947.

Johnson, Angela. *Tell Me A Story Mama*. Orchard, 1989.

Keats, Ezra Jack. *A Letter to Amy*. Harper & Row, 1968.

Lobel, Arnold. *Mouse Tales*. Harper & Row, 1972.

Macaulay, David. *Black and White*. Houghton, 1990.

Oxenbury, Helen. *The Birthday Party*. Dial, 1983.

Paterson, Katherine. *The Tale of the Mandarin Ducks*. Lodestar, 1990.

Rylant, Cynthia. *The Relatives Came*. Bradbury, 1985.

Schwartz, Amy. *Annabelle Swift, Kindergartner*. Orchard, 1988.

Stevenson, James. *The Supreme Souvenir Factory*. Greenwillow, 1987.

Titherington, Jeanne. *A Place for Ben*. Greenwillow, 1987.

Trepov, Mark. *Henry the Explorer*. Little Brown, 1966.

Tressalt, Alvin. *Wake up Farm!* Lothrop, Lee & Shepard, 1955.

Viorst, Judie. *I'll Fix Anthony*. Macmillan, 1988.

Waber, Bernard. *Ira Says Goodbye*. Houghton, 1988.

Waber, Bernard. *Lyle and the Birthday Party*. Houghton, 1972.

Yolen, Jane. *Owl Moon*. Philomel, 1987.

Yorinks, Arthur. *Hey Al*. Farrar, 1986.

Zion, Gene. *Hide & Seek Day*. Harper & Row, 1954.

THE STORY BOOK TREE

Program Purpose: To collect new books, and used books in good condition, to distribute to children who might otherwise not have any.

Program Background: In addition to making our library resources available to everyone who wants them, we strongly believe that a part of developing the reading habit is *ownership* of books. This helps us personalize the experiences that we are able to provide, and is an important step toward developing lifelong readers. This project was designed to be a mechanism for collecting materials that we could then give away. It is especially appropriate for the Christmas/Hanukkah season.

Materials Required: To create the display, we used an artificial tree. It was decorated with "books" made from recycled gift wrap, poster board, holiday cards and construction paper. Collection boxes were recycled cardboard boxes covered with attractive gift wrap. The only other items required were flyers to advertise the program.

IMPLEMENTATION

1. Identify community groups that serve families who would benefit from the program.

2. Identify community groups that would be likely candidates to assist with the delivery of the materials to such places as: Headstart programs, day care centers, health clinics, housing projects, etc.

3. With the information gathered from step two, estimate the number of children who will be receiving books and their ages. Include this information in all promotional materials.

4. Develop partnerships. You might find a local civic organization or a high school service group interested in making the book ornaments, distributing flyers, running collection sites away from the library, and distributing the gift boxes when they are ready.

5. Do all preparation work. Make the ornaments, boxes, create the flyer, etc. (See sample flyers in Chapter 7.)

6. Have a tree decorating party and have the local newspaper photograph it. We kick off the program during Children's Book Week. (Yes, the second week of November is a little early to display a holiday tree! However, we found that we needed the six weeks between Book Week and the Christmas/Hanukkah Holiday to collect the materials needed for our community.) This

program could, of course, be tied in to another time of year that is more suitable in your community.

7. Do a press release for local media, and newsletter articles for any club that is assisting you.

8. Sort books into boxes as they arrive each day. We also put a flyer describing library services in each book.

9. Coordinate delivery of the book collections. We usually distribute between December 15 and December 23.

10. Write thank-you notes to all who assisted in the program.

11. Do a follow-up news story that publicly thanks participants, details how many books were distributed and how many people served. We also announce that we will be doing the project again during the next holiday season.

HINTS FOR A SUCCESSFUL PROGRAM

1. In your publicity, state that the library will make the decisions about the gift materials, and will only distribute those they consider appropriate.

2. Make sure you talk with program directors about the ages and interests of the children they serve. This will assist you in the sorting process. Record this and temporarily tape it to their gift box.

3. Network with corporate librarians. They are able to distribute the flyers in their companies. They may also be able to put a collection box in their staff room or cafeteria for you.

4. Some clubs or companies may be able to give you cash donations. Have a list of titles you'd like to purchase ready for this windfall!

SAMPLE BUDGET

Promotional Flyers	$25.00
Wrappings, ribbons, etc.	25.00
Tree Decorating Party	50.00
Emergency $ if not enough books received	200.00
Thank-yous, certificates, etc.	25.00
Total	**$325.00**

SNOWED INN: STORY HOURS AT THE MALL

Program Purpose: To offer story programs within a public setting in an effort to reach the underserved.

Program Background: There is no doubt that some children seem to be taken everywhere except the library. This was an attempt to reach children bored by their caregiver's holiday shopping, and also to make waiting to see Santa a little more entertaining. This is a good way for the library to reach numerous families who were unaware of the library and its services.

Material Required: Story materials were collected and put into a Story Box that was left at the site. (We kept the box secure by arranging with a bookstore at the mall to keep the box inside their premises during off hours.) Program flyers were designed with the assistance of the mall's management. Some other activities were developed and copied for inclusion in the Story Box. A partnership with a local bookstore provided the books that were raffled off at each session.

IMPLEMENTATION STEPS

1. Contact the management of the mall and set up an appointment to discuss possibilities.

2. Brainstorm possible programs the library could offer and what arrangements the mall will be able to provide. Meet with bookstore representatives to arrange donations as well.

3. Set the calendar and time slots for the programs. Assign staff and volunteer teams to each slot (see Figure 4-4). Prepare orientation.

4. Organize the materials for the Story Box. Get suggestions from staff and volunteers. Materials we have put in the Story Box include books and tapes for the program, a portable tape player, a tip sheet for volunteers, evaluation sheets, and copies of game activities. Game activities we have used include "Winter Bingo," in

---

Figure 4-4 Sign-up Sheet

Anytown Square Snowed Inn
1992 Story Sessions Sign-up Sheet

Sign up in teams: *Time: 10 a.m. - 12 noon*

Nov. 19	Nov. 21	Nov. 23
1._____	1._____	1._____
2._____	2._____	2._____

Nov. 26	Nov. 28	Nov. 30
1._____	1._____	1._____
2._____	2._____	2._____

Dec. 3	Dec. 5	Dec. 7
1._____	1._____	1._____
2._____	2._____	2._____

Dec. 10	Dec. 12	Dec. 14
1._____	1._____	1._____
2._____	2._____	2._____

Dec. 17	Dec. 19	Dec. 21
1._____	1._____	1._____
2._____	2._____	2._____

which the children matched winter pictures to a game card; coloring sheets; song sheets on easy-to-learn songs.

5. Visit the site and take notes on its features to share with staff.

6. Hold staff and volunteer orientation meeting to discuss procedures (see Figure 4-5).

7. Invite local day care centers and nursery schools to attend special sessions scheduled for them at the mall. Confirm all responses. (Figures 4-6 and 4-7)

8. Pick up donations of books from the bookstore and leave the Story Box at the mall—if previously arranged.

Figure 4-5 Procedures for the Mall

Memo: To Snowed Inn Story Readers

From: Marcia Trotta

Re: Procedures for the Mall

1. The "Story Box" for Snowed Inn will be stored at the Mall Bookland. When you do the stories, stop in there and their staff will show you where it is.

2. The giveaway books are being kept in the Children's Library. One team member should get a book before the date of the reading.

3. While we will have a few books in the box, please visit the Children's department and we will help you select some reading materials.

4. There will be mats down in the story area, so the children will feel comfortable on the floor. There will be a white wicker story chair available for you. You should arrive 15 minutes before your program is scheduled to begin to complete set-up.

5. Fill out the form below and return it to me when you are done.

6. Have a great time!! This really is fun!

Date: _____

Time: _____

Readers' names: _____

Number of children participating: _____

Adults: _____

Problems/suggestions: _____

9. Issue a press release about the service and arrange to distribute flyers provided by the mall.

10. Hold the programs. Be prepared to evaluate programs on a regular basis.

11. Send thank-yous to all participants.

12. From the information gathered on the raffle for the donated books (one raffle per session), send a letter and library application to each child (see Figure 4-8).

Figure 4-6 Invitation Flyer

Main Street Public Library Presents:
Story Hour
at
The Anytown Square

Tuesday, November 27   10 a.m.
                             11 a.m.

Tuesday, December 4   10 a.m.
                             11 a.m.

Tuesday, December 11   10 a.m.
                             11 a.m.

If you would like to bring your class to one of these sessions, please return this form with your *1st* and *2nd* choice of date and time *ASAP*. Space is limited and we will notify you of your time.

REGISTRATION IS REQUIRED.

Teacher's Name _____ #_____

School/ Program:

Number of children in class: _____

1st choice of Date _____ Time _____

2nd choice of Date _____ Time _____

Mail to Marcia Trotta, Main Street Public Library:

105 Main Street, Anytown, CT 06450

Figure 4-7 Confirmation Notice

Main Street Public Library
Story Hour
at
The Anytown Square

Sponsor:

Organization:

You are confirmed to bring _____ children on _____ at _____ a.m.

See you there!

Marcia Trotta
Director of Children's Services

Figure 4-8 Follow-up Letter to Children

Main Street Public Library
105 Main Street
Anytown, CT 06540

Dear:_____

We are glad that you had the chance to participate in "Snowed Inn" at the Anytown Square. Did you know that we have similar programs year round at the library?

We are sending along an application for a library card, as well as our upcoming Calendar. Everything we do at the library is free of charge.

We hope you and your parents will drop in soon to see us.

Sincerely,

Marcia Trotta,
Director of Children's Services

STORY TIMES

The staff of the Children's Library will be offering seasonal storytimes at the Meriden Square during the holiday season. Look for us every TUESDAY and FRIDAY morning at 10:30 a.m., and every SATURDAY at 1:30 p.m., and again at 3:00 p.m. This program begins on November 24, and runs through December 23. Call the library for further information at 233-READ.

The Anytown Square has hired fully qualified babysitters for all the days that the Main Street Library will be holding storytime. The hours are Tuesdays and Fridays from 10 a.m. to noon, and Saturdays from 1 to 4 p.m. Various activity toys will be provided by the Early Learning Center. This service is offered free of charge to Anytown Square customers.

HINTS FOR A SUCCESSFUL PROGRAM

1. Thorough planning. Depending upon the way your library is covered, you may need to register this kind of program with an insurance carrier. Make sure the orientation is thorough, and that volunteers know that they must notify the coordinator at least 24 hours in advance if they can't keep their commitment.

2. Prepare people to be flexible. This kind of programming is difficult because you cannot be sure beforehand how many will attend or what age they will be. Make sure everyone who participates has a variety of materials, songs, finger-plays, and other activities to help them deal with variables.

3. To avoid offending anyone's religious beliefs, we steered away from any materials based on religious themes. Instead, we used materials about winter and snow and other favorite stories and songs.

4. We learned to make recommendations to the appropriate staff. During the first year of our program, Santa took a 30 minute break after two hours, and we planned things for the break time. Unfortunately, some parents thought he took his break because of us! Now our program goes on simultaneously with the Santa visits, but in separate locations.

5. Have patience! There are many distractions in doing story hours outside of the library. Learn to work with them, rather than *competing* with them. It helps to remember that the reason we developed this program was somewhat promotional and that the children will get the benefit of more focused story hours when they are brought to the library.

6. Although this program was developed for the Meriden Square Mall, we have adapted it and used the same process with many other organizations and agencies. Some of our other off-site locations included local fast food restaurants (and food stories work out so well here!), the Women, Infants and Children's Program at our local Health Department, city festivals, local parks, community rooms at local housing units. Look around you—there's no end to the possibilities.

7. Program Note: The Meriden Square Mall was recognized with a Maxi Award for sponsoring this program as a community service.

SAMPLE BUDGET

Staff time:	30 hours @ $15.00 average	$450.00
Materials:	Copies, flyers, etc.	100.00
	Wrap-up recognition	
	Party for staff and volunteers:	50.00
	Total	$600.00

OUTREACH TO DAY CARE CENTERS

Program Purpose: To offer story sessions to children who attend day care programs.

Program Background: More and more children are being raised in families where the single caregiver or both parents work full time. The direct result of this is that children are being cared for during the day by someone other than a parent. Parents are able to spend only limited time with their children. Time at home is often spent coping with the everyday chores of survival, and little time is left for reading to children or bringing them to the library. Bringing story hours to day care centers is a way of reaching out to those children who may not have exposure to books and story experience in any other way.

Materials required: Story materials, including books, audiotapes, filmstrips, puppets, and other appropriate audiovisual materials and equipment. Flyers with information about the library to distribute to the children, as well as bookmarks, and library card applications are also needed.

IMPLEMENTATION STEPS

1. Compile a list of day care centers in the community with their addresses and telephone numbers. (This same program can be taken on the road to home-care providers as well. You can obtain a list of these individuals from the state's licensing agency. You might be able to arrange some sort of neighborhood visit, and combine two or more home day care centers. Neighborhood centers, parks, churches are all appropriate locations. We have also included the use of our Bookmobile to help us meet these needs.)

2. Call the director of each center and make an appointment to call on each of them personally.

3. Go to the appointment and discuss the possible programs or resources that might be offered. Find out as much as possible about the families, about the ages of the children, their interests and the on-going program of the center. Visit the room where the programs will take place, and make suggestions about the way it might be arranged for the greatest benefit to the children.

4. Set a regular schedule of attendance at the centers: for instance, every other Monday at 10 a.m.—whatever works for both organizations. You want to make a routine of the library person being there so the children will get used to the idea of books, reading, and the library.

5. If at all possible, assign the same staff person or volunteer to the center each time. This develops a sense of continuity, and the children begin to identify with the "librarian."

6. Contact appropriate media sources to arrange for publicity. A photo of the children listening to stories is a good idea.

7. Try to offer a workshop for parents, aides, and volunteers at the center once, twice, or more often to encourage follow-up activities at home or at the center. Send a letter to parents like the one in Figure 4-9.

8. As coordinator, be sure to get feedback from the volunteer/staff, *and* from the teacher/day care provider. This will help assure that you are offering quality service.

Figure 4-9 Letter to Parents

Main Street Public Library
105 Main Street
Anytown, CT 06450

Dear Parent:

Your child had the opportunity to hear stories told or read by a librarian from the Main Street Public Library today. We had a wonderful time presenting the program and feel that the children enjoyed the stories very much. Such experiences are the basis for a lifelong habit of literacy and learning. We are sending home some information about the library with your child. We have made every effort to offer a wide range of services at hours that will fit busy schedules. We hope that you will be able to drop by soon and visit with us, so that we can show you first hand what the library has to offer your children and you.

Very truly yours,

Marcia Trotta
Director of Children's Services

Send this letter together with a flyer like the one in Figure 8-3 in Chapter 8 and a library card application.

---

9. Send thank-you notes to the centers/teachers for their hospitality.

HINTS FOR A SUCCESSFUL PROGRAM

1. Keep your contacts current. Be sure to check in regularly with the administrators of the centers.

2. Well-trained staff is a must. Remember, they are representing the library.

3. Be consistent and fair. If you are offering your services to one center, you must endeavor to offer them to all. Be sure that you can keep up with the demand once the program is underway.

4. Keep the materials varied. As with any good story program, you will want to be prepared and have a good variety of materials for the program.

SAMPLE BUDGET

Staff Time: 3 hours/week x 52 weeks @ $15/hr.	$2,340.00
Copies of flyers,	
Card applications, book lists, etc.	100.00
Thank yous, certificates, misc.	50.00
Library materials (already in collection)	5,000.00
Total	**$7,490.00**

INTERGENERATIONAL MODEL: YOUNG MOTHERS

Program Purpose: To provide a model for parent-child bonding through literature.

Program Background: Recent studies have indicated that there is a dramatic increase in the number of births to teenage mothers. At the same time, other studies point to the overwhelming importance of the mother's education to her children's academic performance. Because of the rise in teenage pregnancies, the U.S. faces an ever-harder task of making sure all children are ready for school. A teenage mother tends to end her education; only one-half of females who have children before they are 18 have high school diplomas by the time they are in their mid-20s. The library can be a catalyst for the mother to continue her education, as well as a resource to help her contact agencies that will assist her. Research has shown that family literacy programs help increase adult literacy.

Materials Required: A variety of materials, in a variety of formats, that would be appropriate to the audience's interests and needs. Bookmarks, program flyers, gift books for story bags.

IMPLEMENTATION STEPS

1. Contact the school system to learn what programs are in place to encourage teenage mothers to stay in school. Contact the program coordinator and discuss possible partnerships.

2. Consult with any other related agency about reaching this targeted population. Some suggestions are health clinics, area hospitals, Women, Infants, Children Nutrition programs (WIC), among others. Brainstorm with the program coordinator about possible ways to interact with these moms (Worksheets 3-1a and 3-1b in chapter 3 will be very useful for this process).

3. Once you have made these contacts, you should have enough information to make some program determinations. Your decisions will be based on the number of people who need service, and how captive an audience they are. For instance, if they are involved in completing their high school diploma, you may be able to construct a weekly program as part of their language arts requirement. In they are not, you will need to schedule programs at locations that they frequent. Examples include the health clinic or the WIC check distribution office.

4. Also contact local businesses or service clubs to get their help. This may be to recruit some volunteers to assist you with the programs, or for cash to buy materials.

5. One of the reinforcement pieces that I like to provide is a story bag for them to take home and keep. This would include a selection of picture books, hint sheets on how to use the books, or other activities to do. For example, with the book *A Very Hungry Caterpillar*, I would include (a) a soft caterpillar puppet that unzips and turns into a butterfly; (b) a coloring sheet of butterflies; and (c) a simple pattern to make a butterfly from tissue paper and pipe cleaner. The bag also contains library flyers, a library card, and other information that will help. Being able to pay for this is one of the reasons we asked for cash in item 4, above.

6. We have found that traditional story hours for the children (even if they are infants) are number one in popu-

larity with young mothers. We designed these as participatory for the parent and the child. The second most popular programs are demonstrations for the young mothers. For example, to teach counting, we have used Donald Crews' *Ten Black Dots*. We gave the mothers a number of black dots cut from construction paper as well as other objects and showed them how to use these to count. The mothers like to take these experiences and repeat them at home (see chapter 7 for specific activities).

7. Follow up the programs. Perhaps you can send a note to the mother thanking her for her participation. Suggest some other programs/books that you feel she might like. Let her know that the library is a place that cares about her and her child.

Figure 4-10 Sample Letter to Mother

> **Main Street Public Library**
> **105 Main Street**
> **Anytown, CT 06540**
>
> Dear Mom,
>
> Thank you for attending the Baby and Mom program at the Main Street Public Library on Tuesday. We enjoyed having you here and hope you will join us again soon.
>
> Meanwhile, enjoy the materials in the story bag!
>
> Sincerely,
>
>
> Marcia Trotta
> Children's Librarian

HINTS FOR A SUCCESSFUL PROGRAM

1. Keep the programs simple, but practical.
2. Be supportive. It is not useful to be critical; concern and pity are not the same thing.

3. If at all possible, try to have materials available for these families to keep. Chances are that they do not have income to spend on books, but having books in the home is a motivation to read.

4. Do these programs on a regular basis, year round. Different people are having babies all the time, so the audience will be changing.

SAMPLE BUDGET

Storyteller 2hr/mo @ $15/hr x 12 mos	$360.00
Story bags (bags, books, flyers, etc.)	
100 @ $10 each	1,000.00
Postage, stationery, misc.	25.00
Total	**$1,385.00**

INTEGRATION MODEL: SENIORS

Program Purpose: To provide an intergenerational reading experience for people within the community.

Program Background: Our twentieth century society's mobility means many children do not have grandparents living nearby as did previous generations. Likewise, the senior population may not have their children/grandchildren nearby. The natural connections of these age groups have become stretched or broken because of this, and both age groups are poorer for it. Research has shown that intergenerational programs yield tremendous benefits to both age groups.

Materials Required: Reading materials, program flyers, assorted craft materials, refreshments.

IMPLEMENTATION STEPS

1. Contact the local senior center, department of aging, residential housing areas for seniors, and nursing homes to discuss the possibility of beginning an intergenerational program with them.

2. Brainstorm about the kinds of programs that could be offered, their time and frequency. Special attention should be given to the number of seniors and any limitations that they may have such as mobility, sight, diet, or other concerns.

3. Contact local day care centers, nursery schools, and kindergartens, to discuss the possibility of an intergenerational program. You will want to determine whether they are interested, how many children they have and their ages. Are they willing to make arrangements to have their students visit the senior facilities? How often?

4. Once the need is determined, set a schedule with all appropriate individuals.

5. Arrange to have some refreshments following the program. These might include juice, cookies, fruit. It is important that you *know* the limitations of the individuals before you plan these!

6. Develop programs that would appeal to this mixed age group. These might be seasonal favorites—baseball, during the World Series, or stories that would give the seniors an opportunity to share their experiences. Music is important too.

7. Take photographs of the seniors and the children.

8. Know in advance when you will return to do another session, so that they can plan on it.

9. Take a selection of books charged out to the facility and arrange to have staff assist you in lending these. If you have a bookmobile service, this would be an appropriate stop.

10. Have other information about the library with you on these visits.

HINTS FOR A SUCCESSFUL PROGRAM

1. Make sure that you find out all you can about the participants.

2. Choose your story materials carefully.

3. Spend time socializing with the participants. This will help you learn a little more about them, and your future programs might be able to use their talents.

4. Occasionally, plan an activity for the adults to do with the children. This can be a simple craft that they will be able to keep as a reminder of their time together.

5. For the photographs—polaroids work best because you can give them to the children and seniors right away. If your budget doesn't allow for them however, have the film developed at an outlet that offers two prints for the price of one. Send them to the centers or deliver them at your next session.

SAMPLE BUDGET

Storyteller: 2hrs/mo @ $15/hr x 12 mos	$360.00
Refreshments	100.00
Film/Processing	300.00
Misc. flyers, programs	25.00
Total	$785.00

SUGGESTIONS FOR PROGRAM FOLLOW-UP ACTIVITIES

1. Use a tape recorder and have the adults and children tell about something special they remember.

2. Write or draw their favorite things. Provide paper, markers, and crayons. Categories might include: book, song, place, game, food, holiday.

3. Have a sing-along with piano or guitar accompaniment. Old favorites like "A Bushel and a Peck," "Yankee Doodle," and "She's Coming 'Round the Mountain," are easy for the children to follow and a delight for the seniors to remember.

4. If the facility is appropriate, make a treat—cookies are always fun! Provide a written recipe so that the children can take it home. Share the treats.

5. *If* the children are old enough, and if the seniors can handle it, play some games of the past. Hopscotch may be a possibility, as would marbles or jacks.

6. Have lap-time reading. Match the children with a senior and have them choose a story to share together.

7. As a group project, design and decorate a display or bulletin board with photos of the sessions, as well as samples from the activities. Recreation workers and

teachers are always happy to have this type of display and might be willing to assist you.

8. With older children, using old photographs and discussing how times have changed, and oral histories, are wonderful fun.

9. Take turns reading aloud if the child is old enough.

10. Senior and ten- to 13-years-old can write a poem together and read poems together.

SUGGESTIONS FOR INTERGENERATIONAL READING

Ackerman, Karen. *The Song and Dance Man*. Knopf, 1988.

Bunting, Eve. *The Wednesday Surprise*. Clarion, 1989.

Cooney, Barbara. *The Island Bay*. Viking, 1988.

Cooney, Barbara. *Miss Rumphius*. Viking, 1982.

Levinson, Riki. *I Go with My Family to Grandma's*. Dutton, 1986.

Levinson, Riki. *Watch the Stars Come Out*. Dutton, 1985.

HOSPITAL PACKETS FOR NEW PARENTS

Program Purpose: To inform new parents of materials that the library has to assist them in their new role as parents, as well as to inform them of the services that there are for children.

Program Background: Many people, when faced with the new responsibility of raising a child, are overwhelmed by the process. The library is a resource that can assist them through its collection of books, videos, and audiocassettes. They also can be informed of the services that the library offers to children, so they can enroll them as early as possible.

IMPLEMENTATION STEPS

1. Contact all area hospitals and inquire about any special program they may have for new parents. Make an appointment to meet with their program director.

2. Discuss with the program director/s the idea of providing information packets to new parents. Ask for their suggestions on what to include and when the packets should be distributed.

3. Formalize the contents of the packet. This would include bibliographies of appropriate materials, application for library cards, bookmark with library hours, booklist of items to read to very young children, and a book (my choice would be *Goodnight Moon*). All will be packed in a carry bag, with library logo.

4. Bring the proposal to a civic group in an attempt to get funding. Perhaps their logo can be on the carry-bag as well. Also, they may be able to provide people to deliver the bags to the hospital.

5. Another facet of the program might be to speak to the parents briefly at a prenatal class, and then socialize informally over refreshments. A few highlights about library service can be presented, and meeting the Children's Librarian may encourage them to bring their child to the library the first time.

6. Follow up with a congratulatory letter when the baby is born.

HINTS FOR A SUCCESSFUL PROGRAM

1. Keep presentations focused and brief.

2. Be sure that all your information and materials are the latest available.

3. Giving the parents the book and the bag usually makes a strong impression. However, if funding is not forthcoming, go ahead and do it with flyers, and bookmarks to supplement the talk. The important thing to remember is to reach these new parents.

4. Sponsor some event that will get them into the library. Perhaps you can include a free ticket for a monthly drawing that would require their presence. Again, a prize could be a book, or perhaps a soft toy.

Figure 4-11 Letter to New Parents

Main Street Public Library
105 Main Street
Anytown, CT 06540

Dear _____:

Congratulations on the arrival of your new baby!

We share your excitement in nurturing this new person. We hope that the materials we provided in the Parents-to-Be class are helpful. Please call on us if there is a specific information need that we can fill.

We are looking forward to having you visit us. Bring the enclosed ticket with you and enter our free drawing for a set of Beatrix Potter Books and the Peter Rabbit music box.

Looking forward to assisting you in raising your child to be a lifetime reader.

Sincerely,

Marcia Trotta
Director of Children's Services

SAMPLE BUDGET

Postage	$58.00
Flyers, bookmarks, misc.	25.00
Books: 200/yr @ $4.95	990.00
Bags: 200/yr @ $3.00	600.00
Staff Time 1 mo @ $15/hr	180.00
Refreshments/paper goods	100.00
Total	**$1,953.00**

FIRST BOOKS FOR PARENTS TO READ ALOUD

Brown, Margaret Wise. *Goodnight Moon*. Harper, 1947.

Charo, Kate. *The Baby's Bedtime Book*. Dutton, 1984.

Hill, Eric. *Baby Bear's Bedtime*. Random, 1984.

Margallo, Jean. *Close Your Eyes*. Drol, 1978.

Ormerod, Jan. *Moonlight*. Lothrop, 1982.

Orenbury, Helen. *Good Night, Good Morning*. Greenier, Row, 1980.

Zolotow, Charlotte. *The Sleepy Book*. Lothrop, 1958.

BOOKS TO SHARE WITH SIBLINGS

Aliki. *Welcome Little Baby*. Greenier: Row, 1987.

Keats, Ezra Jack. *Peter's Chair*. Harper & Row, 1962.

Ormerod, Jan. *101 Things to Do with a Baby*. Lathrop, 1984.

Vigna, Judith. *Couldn't We Have a Turtle Instead*. Whitman, 1975.

Zolotow, Charlotte. *But not Billy*. Harper & Row, 1983.

BOOKS FOR PARENTS

Bird, Joseph. *To Live as a Family*. Doubleday, 1982.

Chess, Stella. *Know Your Child*. Basic Books, 1987.

Hotchnec, Tracie. *Childbirth and Marriage: The Transition to Parenthood*. Avon, 1988.

Jones, Claudia. *Parents Are Teachers Too*. Williamson, 1988.

Trelease, Jim. *The New Read Aloud*. Penguin, 1989.

Time-Life. *Your Baby's First Year*. Time-Life, 1986.

HOSPITAL OUTREACH HOSPICE PROGRAM

Program Purpose: To provide resource materials for families to use to help children cope with death and dying.

Program Background: Families who are facing the passing of a loved one need support. If children who are experiencing this difficulty can read about children who have encountered death and have coped, they may be comforted. These books might also become the starting point for the adult to talk about the problem with the child.

IMPLEMENTATION STEPS

1. Contact the local hospital and any other organization with hospice services. Make an appointment to meet with a social worker, or counselor who works directly with families of patients.

2. Bring samples of materials that the library owns and discuss the need for these families to have access to the materials.

3. Consider lending a collection of library materials to the hospice for use by families while they are visiting the patient. A browsing collection that would appeal to a broad age range is appropriate, with some titles related to the situation at hand. It is difficult for families under stress and time constraints to make the visit to the library.

4. Compile a booklist of materials that would be useful to help children understand death. Be sure to include library hours. Make copies of the list and leave it in the waiting room along with the circulating collection. Update the list regularly.

5. Develop a relationship with the hospice staff so they will be comfortable calling you with special requests for materials.

6. Talk to a business or community group about funding a project that includes giving away copies of some titles.

HINTS FOR A SUCCESSFUL PROGRAM

1. Review your lists regularly and update with new titles as needed.
2. Be flexible with your loan periods. It may be necessary to adjust these to accommodate people at the hospice.
3. People who use this service are very appreciative of it, and I have found that they often want to thank the library in some way. If you have a gift donation program in place, perhaps you can explain it to the counseling staff, and they will pass on the information if they feel it is appropriate (see Figure 4-12).

HELPING CHILDREN COPE WITH DEATH

Nonfiction

Bernstein, Joanne. *When People Die*. (Grades K-3) Dutton, 1977.

Coerr, Eleanor. *Sadako and the Thousand Paper Cranes*. (Grades 2-5) Putnam, 1972.

Cohn, Janice. *I Had a Friend Named Peter*. (Grades 2-5) Morrow, 1987.

Krementz, Jill. *How it Feels when a Parent Dies*. (Grades 4+) Knopf, 1981.

Marsoli, Lisa. *Things to Know about Death and Dying*. (Grades 3+) Knopf, 1981.

Richter, Elizabeth. *Losing Someone You Love*. (Grades 6+) Putnam, 1986.

Simon, Norma. *The Saddest Time*. (Grades 1+) Whetman, 1986.

Stein, Sarah. *About Dying*. (Grades 1+) Walker, 1974.

Fiction

Aliki. *The Two of Them*. (Grades ps-2) Mulberry, 1987.

Brown, Margaret Wise. *The Dead Bird*. (Grades ps-2) W.R. Scott, 1988.

De Paola, Tomie. *Nana Upstairs, Nana Downstairs*. (Grades ps-3) Putnam, 1973.

Figure 4-12 Contribution to the Library Form

**Main Street Public Library
Give a Book to the Library Program**

This form is for the convenience of our library patrons who are interested in participating in our "Give a Book to the Library Program."

Its purpose is twofold:

1. To enable the library to expand the resources that are available to our community.

2. To give our patrons the opportunity to present a visible gift in honor of or in memory of a relative or friend.

Name(s) of donor(s): _____

Address: _____

      # and street

      _____

      city state zip

I/We wish to contribute $_____ for the:

    ( ) Purchase of a book on the subject of_____
    ( ) Purchase of a book on a subject identified by the library staff.

Each book added to the library will carry a bookplate. Please indicate how you would like that bookplate to read: _____ _____

Please send an announcement of my/our donation to:

Name(s) _____

Address: _____

      # and street

      _____

      city state zip

Please make checks payable to the Main Street Public Library. If you need further information, please call 238-2344 ext. 23.

An acknowledgment of the gift will be sent to both the donor and the honoree or their family.

Gackenbach, Dick. *Do You Love Me?* (Grades K-4) Seabury, 1975.

Jordan, Mary Kate. *Losing Uncle Tim.* (Grades 2-5) A. Whitman, 1989.

Mann, Peggy. *There Are Two Kinds of Terrible.* (Grades 5+) Doubleday, 1977.

Martin, Ann. *With You and Without You.* (Grades 5+) Holiday House, 1986.

Viorst, Judith. *The Tenth Good Thing About Barney.* (Grades K-4) Atheneum, 1971.

Wilhelm, Hans. *I'll Always Love You.* (Grades ps-3) Crown, 1985.

These books and others are available at the Main Street Public Library 238-2344. Hours: Monday—Thursday 10 a.m. - 9 p.m.; Friday—Saturday 10 a.m. - 5 p.m.

HOMEWORK ACTIVITY CENTER

Program Purpose: To provide an environment for children who need assistance with their homework.

Program Background: The library staff noticed a steady increase of use by school children between 3 and 6 p.m. every weekday. These children live within walking distance or attend a school within walking distance and walk to the library after the session is over. These large numbers of unattended children began to demand too much attention from the staff in terms of homework help and discipline, to the extent that the librarians became overburdened. An idea evolved that would creatively channel the energies of the children and teach them how to use their time efficiently: a homework assistance program.

IMPLEMENTATION METHODS

1. Talk to the children and determine what needs they have (see Worksheet 4-1 for some sample questions to ask).

2. Discuss the idea of a homework center with appropriate community agencies and government officials. Those to include are the school administrators—both public and private; social service agencies such as the YWCA/YMCA, Boys/Girls Clubs, Literacy Volunteers, day care coordinators, town officials, such as the security and risk administrator, and the Community Development administrator. Use the feedback to determine if this need is recognized by them and get their support.

3. Develop the idea into a proposal that elaborates on the program's purpose, and the requirements necessary to establish the program (see the sample proposal and cover letter in Figures 4-13 and 4-14).

4. Once the funding is secured, order any equipment and/or supplies that you listed in the proposal.

5. Recruiting volunteers is the next step. Cooperation with a Literacy Volunteer program is effective. Applications to be a volunteer can be placed in public places like the "Y" or schools. The newspaper might do a story on the project and include a call for volunteers.

6. Volunteer training should be carefully planned—see more detailed suggestions in Chapter 6. Training sessions for volunteer tutors might include a tour of the children's section, an explanation of how to use the on-line catalog, a review of the children's computer software, and an overview of basic reference tools such as encyclopedias and dictionaries. The volunteers should be taught how to identify a slow reader, how to offer positive suggestions to the children, and how to help them improve their study skills. A handout with a list of "Homework Helpers," such as the one in Figure 4-15, is useful for both volunteers and students.

7. Schedule the volunteers. We found that they took their assignments more seriously when they were posted with a given time commitment.

WORKSHEET 4-1

QUESTIONS TO ASK CHILDREN ABOUT THE HOMEWORK CENTER:

1. Do you come to the library after school without an adult?

   If yes, how may days a week? What days?

2. What are you looking for when you come to the library?

   A place to wait for parents to pick you up: _____
   Reference materials for reports: _____
   A place to meet with your friends: _____
   Help with school work: _____
   Other: _____

3. If the library were to have adults available who could help you with your homework, would you ask them for help?

   Yes_____ No_____
   What subjects: _____

4. How often do you get homework in your class? Do you need someone to help you do it?

5. Is there someone at home who is able to help you with your work. If not, do you know about the program that is here at the library to help adults (Literacy Volunteers)?

   At this juncture, you may choose to send them home with some information about programs for their parents.

6. Is there any other way that the library can help you?

Figure 4-13 Program Proposal Cover Letter

Main Street Public Library
105 Main Street
Anytown, CT 06450

```
Joanne Miller
Director of Human Resources
The XYZ Corporation
One Corporation Park
Anytown, CT 06450

Dear Ms. Miller:

I would like to thank you for giving me the opportunity
to talk with you about the Children's Library.

As you suggested, I have developed a proposed plan for
a Homework Activity Center for your review. I think
that it outlines our intentions. Please feel free to
call me if you have any questions.

I am excited about the possibilities that this project
would allow, and I appreciate your assistance with it.

Sincerely,


Marcia Trotta
Director of Children's Services
```

---

8. Have the volunteers sign in and sign out. This is important because it gives you a record of who worked on specific days. It is also an important security check. For emergency purposes, the staff must know who is in the library. Having them wear identifying badges is a good idea as well.

9. Maintain a close rapport with the volunteers. One staff member should be assigned to be their supervisor. This will help you sustain high-quality tutoring. It will also provide a means of getting feedback about the program so that it can be constantly improved.

10. Publicize the service if you are able to meet the demand. This will not only let the community know what you are offering, it will bring in students and more volunteers.

Figure 4-14 Sample Homework Center Proposal

Main Street Public Library
105 Main Street, Meriden 06450
Contact: Marcia Trotta - (203) 238-5000

PROPOSAL: HOMEWORK ACTIVITY CENTER

Purpose of the Program: The library is interested in providing service to children who need help with their homework.

Program Background: The library staff is aware that there is a growing number of unattended children who are in the facility after school. The library staff is not able to keep up with the demands of this group of children who need constant attention. There are 75 to 125 children per day who are in the library alone from 3 to 6 p.m. Some of them may live within walking distance. The majority, however, go to school within walking distance and are waiting for a parent to pick them up after work.

Program Description: The library would offer the services of a Homework Activity Center on a daily basis. This Center would be staffed with volunteers who will assist children with their assignments. They might also just listen to them and talk with them so that the children are occupied and therefore less likely to become discipline problems. This program would be in keeping with the library's mission to be an information center for people of all ages.

PROGRAM NEEDS

Volunteers:
1. We feel that the library would need to have the center staffed three hours a day (3-6 p.m.) five days a week, plus five hours on Saturday, for a total of 20 hours.
2. We feel that two volunteers on duty at a time would be the most effective. There will be a need for 40 volunteer-hours.
3. Recruitment: The library will recruit these volunteers through various means, including newspaper articles and radio shows, school visits, and contacts with other agencies.
4. All volunteers will attend a thorough volunteer training program organized and executed by the Children's Librarian.
5. Volunteers will not be paid but will be invited to attend a recognition reception.

(continued)

Figure 4-14 Sample Homework Center Proposal   (Cont.)

Main Street Public Library
105 Main Street, Meriden 06450
Contact: Marcia Trotta - (203) 238-5000

Cash Donations:

The library needs $4,000.00 to begin this program.
In-kind Services Needed:
  1. Printing Services: The library will develop information flyers about the Homework Activity Center and volunteer recruitment forms. We need 200 recruitment forms and 1,000 promotional flyers printed.
  2. For the volunteer recognition program, it would be nice to give them a small gift. Estimated 100 per year of an item of jewelry made by your company.

ITEMIZED BUDGET: YEAR 1

Furniture (study carrels)	$1,200.00
Mac Classic Computer with printer:	1,350.00
Supplies (ribbons, paper, etc.)	500.00
Software	300.00
Additional Library Materials	500.00
Volunteer Recognition	150.00
Total	$4,000.00

At this time, The XYZ Corporation is the only source that the library is approaching for funding. This will give us the opportunity to provide special recognition with a plaque to them. The library will be contributing an equal amount through the use of its staff and the overhead of the building, yearly.

ITEMIZED BUDGET: YEAR 2

Mac Classic Computer with printer:	$1,350.00
Supplies (ribbons, paper, etc.)	500.00
Additional Library Materials	500.00
Volunteer Recognition	150.00
Total	$2,500.00

Figure 4-15 Homework Helpers

423   *Dictionaries* that can be taken out.

372.6 Be   *Help Is On the Way for Book Reports* by Marilyn Berry. Explains the steps used in writing a book report, including choosing a book, identifying the theme, and writing the report.

372.4 Be   *Help Is On the Way for Reading Skills* by Marilyn Berry. Provides helpful hints for reading, understanding what you read, and getting the most out of your reading.

372.1 Be   *Help Is On the Way for Schoolwork* by Marilyn Berry. Gives hints on how to organize homework and improve study habits.

372.6 Be   *Help Is On the Way for Written Reports* by Marilyn Berry. Explains the steps used in writing a report, including choosing a topic, doing research, making an outline, and writing the final draft.

428.1 Da   *How to Improve your Spelling and Vocabulary* by Jessica Davidson. In a clear, readable, and humorous style, the author provides many ways to help you build your spelling and vocabulary skills.

502.8 We   *How to Do a Science Project* by David Webster. Suggestions for three types of science projects —report, demonstration, and research, with emphasis on procedures used to do a successful research project.

421 Ga   *How to Stop a Sentence and other Methods of Managing Words* by Nora Gallagher. Uses a humorous touch to explain the use of different punctuation marks.

371.3 Wi   *How to Study and Learn* by Janet Wikler. Offers guidelines for improving learning and study skills, such as taking tests and memorizing; and suggests ways to deal with emotional interference.

507 Be   *So You Want to Do a Science Project* by Joel Beller. A guide to selecting, researching and carrying out a science project—complete with suggestions for more than 100 projects.

421 Wo   *World Book Complete Word Power Library.* Includes the skills and techniques needed to develop your ability to use both the written and spoken word.

HINTS FOR A SUCCESSFUL PROGRAM

1. Continuity is important for children. Have the volunteers schedule themselves for the same time and same day of the week.

2. Have the volunteers make a time commitment when they are recruited. Two to three hours a week is fair, and is worth your investment of time in training them.

3. Train the volunteers well, and update their training as it becomes necessary.

4. Keep the volunteers informed about library happenings. You need to work at making them feel part of the library.

5. Reward the volunteers. Perhaps a reception can be held with certificates or other tokens of your appreciation awarded at this time.

6. Improve the program through feedback, addition of new materials and training.

7. Invite the public to an open house to show the facility where the Homework Activity Center is located. If there have been sponsors, invite them as well and honor them with a plaque or certificate for their contribution.

8. Remember also to keep the sponsor updated about the Center. It may be that they will make further donations or they may have staff who would be interested in volunteering.

RECOGNITION FOR THE DONOR

Public recognition can be in the form of a letter to the editor, and/or a presentation of a plaque for the donor's office. Formal thank-you letters must be written to the donor's leadership, as well as personal thank-you notes to all people who assisted you in developing the program.

Printed Material

1. Develop a bookmark with the hours of the homework center and its services. It will have a message that the Center is a project of The XYZ Corporation, and it will carry the Center's logo.

BACK TO SCHOOL

The Children's Library has a wide assortment of reference materials and informational books that are suitable for children's homework assignments. Stop in and ask the staff for help in choosing the right book for you.

CHILDREN'S LIBRARY

Main Street Public Library

105 Main Street

233-READ

2. Enlarge the bookmark to poster size and put these up in strategic locations throughout the town.

3. All printed library materials that are purchased with the grant monies should carry a special bookplate, with the words "Gift of The XYZ Corporation" on them.

Visible Recognition

1. Place a plaque in the area of the library that houses the Homework Center that reads: *XYZ Corporation Homework Activity Center*.

2. Plan a grand opening with a reception to which members of the community will be invited. A brief presentation will outline the goals of the center.

Public Relations/Publicity

1. Have a photo taken in the Homework Activity Center of representatives of the donor. Make it available along with all press releases.

2. Send a press release to local papers, radio, cable stations, and television stations along with the photo. Offer to be interviewed about the project.

3. Write feature articles for the Friends of the Library Newsletter, the Board of Education Newsletter, and the statewide library association newsletter.

4. Visit schools to inform educators about the program. Offer to speak to parent organizations so they are aware of this service as well.

EVALUATION AND ACCOUNTABILITY

1. Accountability should be fulfilled with a written report that documents all expenses. The purpose of the report is to summarize the effectiveness of the project and how it is meeting its goals based on the evaluations.

2. Carry out evaluations in four different arenas. Using the forms in Chapter 6, the staff can provide an observation evaluation. Keep accurate records concerning the number of hours the center was staffed by volunteers, and the number of students who used the services. Ask the volunteers to fill out the evaluation form

as well. In addition to their views on the effectiveness of the program, we would also ask them for feedback on whether they feel their time was well spent. We will also ask for feedback from the community agencies, educators, and parents. But most important of all, we will talk with the children who use the services and ask for their input on how we can improve the Center and services as well as their comments on how it may have helped them.

HOSPITAL VISITS

Program Purpose: To visit children who are hospitalized and provide them with library services.

Program Background: Children who are hospitalized, especially for extended periods of time, are not able to take advantage of the library services being offered within their communities. This project is designed to bring them library materials for pleasure reading, to make them aware of materials they could read concerning their hospitalization, and to provide them with a community visitor who cares about their welfare.

Materials Required: Library books that can be shared with children of different ages, books that can be left with the children permanently, handouts such as bookmarks.

IMPLEMENTATION STEPS

1. Call the social services department at the hospital. Ask for an appointment with them, or with the appropriate staff to discuss the project idea.
2. During the appointment, determine the child census, and whether that number remains relatively constant. You should also inquire whether these patients are there for long-term care, or short stays. You will need to set up a system to provide this information every time you plan this program.

3. You will also need to know whether there are physical limitations so you can determine what types of materials the children will be able to use. If they are restrained, they may not be able to turn pages. If they have sight problems, they may need audio material instead of books.

4. You will also need to discuss the best time of day to make the visits so you do not interfere with medical care.

5. If there is a recreation area, you might consider leaving a collection of materials for use there.

6. Once the needs are determined, draw up a proposal concerning the supply of books you will need to give to the patients. You should then contact a local civic group or business and request their support.

7. Once you determine the frequency of the program, you may need to recruit some volunteers who will assist the staff in offering it on a regular basis.

8. As with other programs, evaluate frequently to be sure the program continues to meet the needs of your target population.

HINTS FOR A SUCCESSFUL PROGRAM

1. Make sure staff and volunteers are especially well-trained and able to cope with the sometimes distressing situations that they are sure to encounter.

2. Know who to contact in the event that the child needs medical help. At no time should the staff intervene.

3. Choose selections carefully. The materials that are most successful in this situation are pleasurable stories.

4. Be sensitive to the hospital's schedule, and the flexibility it may require of you.

SAMPLE BUDGET

Staff 1hr/wk @ $15/hr x 52 wks	$780.00
Materials to give out	750.00
Misc. flyers, bookmarks, etc.	50.00
Total	**$1,580.00**

SUGGESTED TITLES

Elliot, Ingrid. *Hospital Roadmap*. (Ages 4-8) Resources for Children in Hospitals, 1991. A step-by-step guide to the hospital.

Howe, James. *The Hospital Book*. (Ages 7-10) Crown, 1981. A guide to the hospital stay.

Marsoli, Lisa Ann. *Things to Know Before You go to the Hospital*. (Ages 7-12) Silver Burdett, 1981. Clear photographs and accurate description of what to expect.

Reit, Seymour. *Jenny's in the Hospital*. (Ages 4-8) Western Publishing Co., 1984. Simple but reassuring story of a girl's treatment following a bad fall.

Rockwell, Anne. *The Emergency Room*. (Ages 5-8) Macmillan, 1985. Straightforward narrative of care that may be needed following accidents.

Shay, Arthur. *What Happens when You Go to the Hospital*. (Ages 5-10) Reilly & Lee, 1969. A first-person report of a tonsilectomy.

Sobel, Harriet. *The Hospital Story*. (Ages 4-10) Walker, 1974. A parent-child book on hospitals.

Weber, Alfons. *Elizabeth Gets Well*. (Ages 5-8) Crowell, 1970. Picture book that explains unfamiliar things a child sees in a hospital.

STORIES ABOUT HOSPITALS

Bemelmans, Ludwig. *Madeline*. (Ages 3-7) Simon & Schuster, 1939. A story in rhyme about an appendectomy.

Blume, Judy. *Deenie*. (Ages 9-13) Bradbury Press, 1973. Teenage novel about an unexpected operation and adjustment.

Howe, James. *A Night Without Stars*. (Ages 9-13) Atheneum, 1983. Reassuring novel of a young girl's surgery experience.

Marino, Barbara. *Eric Needs Stitches*. (Ages 4-8) Addison-Wesley, 1979. Realistic information in story form.

Martin, Ann. *With You and Without You.* (Ages 9-13) Holiday House, 1986. A 12-year-old's struggle with her father's terminal illness.

Rey, H.A. *Curious George Goes to the Hospital.* (Ages 3-7) Houghton Mifflin, 1966. The mischievous monkey in a hospital adventure.

Tamburine, Jean. *I Think I Will Go to the Hospital.* (Ages 3-7) Abingdon Press, 1965. Reassuring story by a local author.

Wolde, Gunilla. *Betsy and the Doctor.* (Ages 3-6) Random, 1988. Children identify with Betsy and her emergency visit.

5 TECHNIQUES THAT WORK

The ultimate success of your outreach program will depend upon the techniques and the methods you employ to carry it out. Perhaps one of the most encouraging things is that librarians already know the basics from their work with children. The programs will need some fine-tuning in order to meet the needs of the particular situation. The important thing to remember is that outreach work will be successful if you take the time to lay the groundwork for your programs. This will give you a solid foundation on which to build your programs.

It is important that you keep your goals in mind, and employ techniques that help you achieve the goals. You will find that if you develop techniques that help children engage in reading in a personal way, in a welcoming and relaxed atmosphere, it becomes the pleasurable experience that we want it to be. Reading presented with positive expectations will bring pleasure and understanding. You will demonstrate that reading is worth the effort!

TECHNIQUES FOR STORY READING

As professional librarians, we have learned a number of techniques aimed at making reading pleasurable. The good news is that you do not need to learn another set of techniques in order to do outreach work successfully! Some adaptations may be necessary, but I have found that reading picture books aloud, storytelling, and book talking are still our three most often used methods. In addition, we have found on occasion that it is important to be flexible about story extenders. Art projects, creative dramatics, flannel boards, pantomimes, cooking, puppetry, may be appropriate to use. There are may resources available that explain all these in depth. Regardless of what techniques you choose, there are a few basic guidelines that are important to follow.

Planning: Nothing can replace this crucial basic step. Set aside the time you need and organize this with no interruptions. Be familiar with all books, fingerplays, and other activities. Pay attention to the condition of the books you will be using. Rely on the techniques for selecting materials to help you make your choices. Shabby-looking materials will give a poor impression—find good looking copies of your selections. Be familiar with the environment in which you will be doing your story. Try to eliminate any obvious distractions.

Personal Touch: Greet all the children and their caregivers when they arrive for the session. Let them have the time to talk to you and get to know you as a person so that they feel comfortable with you.

Gather the Group: Establish a routine to begin the program. You might like to use a rhyme or a game to take the children to the area where you will be presenting the program. An example would be to form a line and have each child put a hand on the shoulder of the child in front and chant "choo-choo," as they move along.

Introduce the Story: This may be a simple statement telling a little about the book. It gives you a few minutes to get everyone settled, and you can observe the children at the same time.

Pay Attention to the Way You Sound: Your voice should be clear and natural, but animated. Base your volume of sound on the story and use your voice to convey a mood, a dramatic quality, or an emotion. Also, remember to use body language effectively. Smile, use eye contact, and hold the book so everyone can see.

Explain Language as Necessary: There may be some words that are not familiar. Give one or two word definitions and continue on so you don't interrupt the flow of the story.

Anticipate and Prevent Disruptions: You have already planned to set the environment, but the children may be the cause of the disruptions. Use eye contact to help you gauge reactions and spot trouble before it starts. Also call on your "grabbers"— those fingerplays and other participatory activities that are a great device to keep the attention of the audience. Plan for the children to participate—retelling the story, making up their own, doing voices—and let them know they will have this opportunity.

Follow up: Have books available that the children and their parents can borrow. Make it easy for them to get their own library cards. Give them promotional materials about other programs.

TECHNIQUES FOR SELECTING READING MATERIALS

1. Consider the child(ren) for whom you are choosing the book. For them to enjoy it, the book should be appropriate to their age and developmental stage. Try to read the book from the *child's* point of view. You will find that this makes a big difference.

2. Consider the format of the book in judging its appropriateness. Does the action unfold through words and illustrations? Is it well organized? Are the colors clear and bright? Is the content both adequate and accurate?

3. Test the "readability" of the book. Is the subject interesting? Is the book well-written, with flowing language, rhythm and refrains. Are the characters believable? Does the action contain suspense so that it arouses the child's imagination? Does the story make sense? What is the comprehension level of the book?

4. Use a variety of books in your sessions. It is true that children do like to hear some stories repeated over and over, but our responsibility is to expose them to as many different kinds of materials as we can. Consider rebus stories, concept books, folk and fairy tales, and of course, Mother Goose and other poetry selections. Put the reviews aside for a moment! Rely on your own judgment and experience to create a program for the occasion.

5. Your opinion of the materials is very important to the overall success. Do you agree with the values that are presented in the book? Do you like the book? If you are bored by a book, or dislike it, that message will come across as you read. Likewise, so will honest enjoyment. Take the time to select—there are so many possibilities!

TECHNIQUES FOR USING AUDIOVISUAL MATERIALS

While the principal purpose of your reading program is to introduce children and their caregivers to books, sometimes the high quality audiovisual materials that are available in today's market are very useful. In most instances, these function as grabbers, but they can help bridge a language barrier, and often are familiar formats across cultures because of our media-centered society. They are also valuable because of the performers reading them and the enhancements that the format offers. You can select a number of sound recordings, filmstrips, and videos to supplement your program. Your selection techniques would be the same as if you were choosing printed materials, with some additions. Make sure that you check the products for quality of production as well as its adherence to the literature on which it was based.

GENERAL TIPS FOR OUTREACH SERVICES

1. Select people to work in the outreach program who genuinely like children.

2. Select people who are enthusiastic and animated.

3. Emphasize the importance of punctuality, courtesy, flexibility, cooperativeness, and consideration of others.

4. Prepare! Prepare! Prepare! Make sure you know the appropriate way to dress (should you be in jeans or a suit?). Know who is likely to be there, and how many. Have *more* materials than you need.

5. Have fun! Reading is fun and *you* as well as your audience should enjoy it!

TECHNIQUES FOR EVALUATING THE PROGRAMS

Evaluating what you are doing on a regular basis is an important part of keeping your program viable. There will be times when you must be very specific; at other times you will be able to gather information informally. You will want to evaluate on three different levels: first, by observing the children who are participating in the programs; second, by observing the staff who are implementing the programs; and finally, from the perspective of the parents, teachers, and other adults who are available at the off-site locations. The questions that you ask for evaluative purposes should be designed to elicit the kind of feedback you need in order to improve the services you are offering. You will want to ask specific questions about your particular programs. The following worksheets can be used to get an overview of the programs.

WORKSHEET 5-1

OBSERVATION OF CHILDREN DURING STORY SESSIONS

Name of Presenter: _____

Setting: Date: _____   Time: _____

               Location: _____

No. of Children Present: _____   **Est. Audience Age:** _____

Other People Present: _____

Comments: _____

Verbal Responses:

    1. Children asked questions?   Yes_____   No_____

    2. Children able to predict outcome?   Yes_____   No_____

    3. Children repeated words, phrases?   Yes_____   No_____

    4. Children related to events/characters?   Yes_____   No_____

    5. Children asked about a particular event?   Yes_____   No_____

      Which ones? _____

    6. Children reacted to events in story?   Yes_____   No_____

    7. Children asked for book to be read again?   Yes_____   No_____

Nonverbal Responses:

    1. Children imitated actions in the story?   Yes_____   No_____

    2. Children smiled, laughed?   Yes_____   No_____

    3. Children pointed to pictures?   Yes_____   No_____

    4. Children exhibited facial expressions?   Yes_____   No_____

      Other: _____

WORKSHEET 5-2

OBSERVATION BY STAFF

Program Location: _____

Program Date: _____

1. **How many people attended the event?** _____

   Children under 5 _____

   Children 5-10 _____

   Parents _____

   Others _____

2. **How did they react to presentation?**

   Enjoyed it?

   Asked questions?

   Asked for stories to be read again?

   Asked for information about other events?

   Asked for information about the library?

   Other?

3. **How was the set-up?**

   Were things in place?

   Did facility staff expect you?

   Is there anything that needs to be done to improve the alliance?

4. **Suggestions you may have for future programs:**

WORKSHEET 5-3

OBSERVATIONS OF PARENTS AND OTHER ADULTS

Program Location: _____

Date: _____

1. **How did you learn about this program?**

   Flyer   _____

   Poster   _____

   Newspaper   _____

   Radio   _____

   Another Person _____

   Other   _____

2. **What was the best part of the program?**
   Did your child enjoy it as well?

3. **What suggestions do you have for improvement?**

4. **Would you be interested in attending more library programs?**

   Yes:_____   **No:**_____   **Not Sure:**_____

   Which kinds?   _____

   Which days of the week? _____

   What time of the day?   _____

5. **Any additional comments:**

(continued)

WORKSHEET 5-3 (Cont.)

6. If you would like to be placed on our mailing list, you may include your name and address in the box below. NOTE: Your name will not be sold or distributed to any outside database.

Yes! I would like to be placed on the library services/outreach mailing list:

NAME: _____

ADDRESS: _____

CITY/STATE/ZIP: _____

Would you like to help volunteer in any of our programs?:

YES: _____   NOT AT THIS TIME: _____

6 PERSONNEL

DEVELOPING QUALITY OUTREACH STAFF

As with any service, the ultimate success of your outreach program will depend upon the level of understanding and the support it gets from the staff implementing it. In many cases one person, usually the children's librarian, determines that outreach services are necessary. It is this person who begins developing plans about what to offer and where. By definition, outreach services will have to be offered in *as many* off-site areas as possible. Because other individuals—both paid staff and volunteers—will be the ones actually implementing the services, they should become part of the planning as well as the implementing! A vital part of the librarian's role will be to recruit, train, and develop many talented people so that outreach services become a reality.

One of the most important and thorough documents about personnel is the Association for Library Service to Children's (ALSC's) Competencies for Librarians Serving Children in Public Libraries.[1] There are also numerous other lists of recommended competencies available. These lists encompass a broad range of professional skills and expertise that many state agencies and library associations consider basic for all levels of staff who provide services to children and youth. However, I believe that Mathews, Flum and Whitney in "Kids Need Libraries," have most succinctly and most accurately captured the essence of what is the most necessary component:

> Caring about kids and treating them with dignity is essential; it ignites a sense of hope and belief in the future and provides a measure of protection against self-destructive behaviors that often tempt youth.[2]

Children must be treated with respect, and the service provider who understands that *all* children should have free access to *all* library materials and services will be a tremendous asset to any outreach program. Depending on the responsibility level and the involvement level of the various individuals, the librarian can tailor the above mentioned competencies in training. When hiring and recruiting, it is important to keep in mind that the people chosen must possess certain other qualities, in order to fulfill their function in the broader scope of the program. While you will be able to train people in the specifics of the outreach program, there is *no* replacement for a caring, sensitive attitude that marks the ability of one person to respect and reach out to another.

ESSENTIAL PERSONALITY QUALITIES

Empathy: This quality enables a person to imagine him or herself in someone else's situation. Outreach workers have to be able to understand how difficult another's life might be. It is this ability of seeing things from another point of view that makes possible formation of a relationship between the service provider and the clientele. It is quite different from sympathy.

Flexibility: This is the ability to adapt to other environments with little resistance and without losing sight of the goal. Doing outreach often puts people into situations that are very unfamiliar. People must be able to accept situations as they are and not make judgments, nor force their sense of what is "right" onto others. This takes a great deal of self-discipline, as well as tolerance, but does result in non-critical, non-threatening attitudes.

Enthusiasm: A genuine excitement about this type of work is not something you can teach. Yes, it does rub off from *your* attitude, and you can nourish it by your interchanges with participants, but undeniably the vitality of the providers gives the program vitality. People should not be forced to do outreach services if they are not comfortable doing them, even eager to do them. Inevitably a lack of willingness surfaces and will undermine your program! Choose people with a zest for loving children and reading!

Positive Attitude: The staff must have confidence in themselves and must believe that they will be able to make a difference. An upbeat approach is catching and the participants quickly develop a new attitude of their own. When introducing the concept of outreach services and all of its components, guard against making it seem overwhelming. Present the program in sections or components that are "do-able." Nothing succeeds like success, and this approach will keep a positive attitude alive and well.

ESSENTIALS FOR THE COORDINATOR

In addition to the qualities listed above, some other attributes are a *must* for the coordinator of the program:

Vision: Using the environment created by strategic planning, the coordinator must be able to see the broad potential of the program and convey it to others. Simultaneously, the coordinator needs to remain objective, and realistic.

Readiness to Innovate: Creativity is a factor, but in truth, the willingness to take risks is more essential here. Not every plan works, and the coordinator must be able to evaluate, readjust, and forge ahead to meet the goals.

Commitment: The old adage "practice what you preach" is appropriate here! The coordinator is a leader; he or she is the person who pilots the programs and takes a personal responsibility for them, carefully evaluating them before they are delegated to others.

Leadership: Only the experience of having been in the field will prepare the coordinator for supervision of the outreach staff. Communication and interpersonal skills are needed to alert the staff to situations that may present challenges. The coordinator has to be dedicated to directing consistent attention and time to encourage the staff to carry out the program.

SUPPORT STAFF AND VOLUNTEERS

Here are some other areas you will want to address to ensure the success of your program:

Reliability: You want people who will make a commitment and keep to it. Remember, whenever you send someone out to do outreach services that person is representing the library. The effect on the library will be negative if the person is late for scheduled events, or worse yet, misses an event totally.

Adaptability: You will not be with your staff and volunteers most of the time; therefore you must choose people who are going to exhibit common sense. There will be times when they have to make decisions or modify plans. They must be flexible and able to adapt to different social and cultural situations.

Approachability: This is a necessity if we keep the goal of outreach services in mind—to reach all children and their families and caregivers with literature and information. For this match to happen, the good relationship that develops between people is the key. Pleasant, friendly manners and a willingness to listen to what others have to say will make for success.

COMPONENTS FOR A TRAINING PROGRAM

Once you have developed your staffing pool, provide them with orientation about the library's operations, and about the new program. Following are general training components for a well-rounded staff, which you will doubtless have to tailor to reflect your individual situation.

General Knowledge of Child Development: This must cover the mental, physical, cultural and social development of the child. There are some standard benchmarks for what children should able to achieve at given ages within certain environments. There are many good sources to use for this information. If you don't feel competent to teach this material, this is a perfect time to form an alliance! You will find many able people in the community—in preschools, and day care centers, and at local community colleges to name a few. Be sure your staff has the background they need to adapt to children's diverse needs and behaviors.

General Knowledge of Children's Literature: As the librarian, it is your responsibility to keep abreast of all the books and other materials that are available for children. It is also your responsibility to expose the staff and the volunteers to as many of these wonderful items as possible on a regular basis. Provide them with listening experiences! One of my favorite training activities is to read some of the books aloud with them. It gives me a chance to demonstrate some techniques for reinforcement purposes without the process becoming routine. It also gives the group an indication of how adults react to the process and gets them used to the idea that other adults will be listening to them as well. As often as possible, I encourage my bravest volunteers or other staff to do the reading as well. This is a painless way to learn—and we all learn a lot from one another! Don't forget to go over equipment use (puppets, audiovisuals, etc.) to let people know what other resources are available and how they can enhance story programs.

Coping With Crisis: A good training technique is to provide hypothetical case studies of situations that might arise. For example, you could stage incidents in which a fire alarm sounds; a child suffers a seizure; or a child becomes violently disruptive, perhaps, depending on your community, even wielding a weapon. Hands-on opportunities help the staff learn to make difficult decisions. It is always better to be prepared. The trained staff will find it easier to cope in times of crisis.

Familiarity With Library Policies: Everyone working in the program needs to have basic information about the library. Provide them with a complete overview of library rules and policies. While you may think *everyone* knows when the library is open, they don't. If you think they know how to get a library card, they don't always remember all the details! Staff and volunteers need to respect all questions and let the person know that each question is important to them. It is much less frustrating if the staff can answer as many as possible. However, they should be aware that there are some questions they *will not* be able to answer and that is okay. They should assure the person that someone will get back to them with a correct answer A.S.A.P.

Cultivate Their Talents: One of the most wonderful things about people is that they are different! People have so many talents and abilities—the coordinator's job is to determine what these special abilities are and to put them to good use! Not only is it to the program's advantage, but people feel good about themselves when they are in the spotlight and performing at or near their peak! All people are not able to do all jobs—but a successful coordinator will note strengths and weaknesses and match them with the appropriate function.

Roles and Responsibilities: Staff members will feel more comfortable and will be much more productive when they know exactly what is expected of them. Give them specific tasks. Set limits so no one is overwhelmed. Be clear and follow up to be sure that tasks are being completed in a satisfactory manner.

Specific Orientation to Off-Site Location: This should be done in small groups or one-to-one if need be. The staff must become familiar with the site *before* their first working visit. Check out the parking, the physical space, lighting, furniture, equipment, etc. You should schedule an appointment for both of you with a contact person at the site, clarifying its purpose, their role, and the library's role. This will give them the background they need to ask questions of the host.

WHERE TO RECRUIT VOLUNTEERS

There are people in all walks of life who are willing to give some time if you explain your needs carefully. Some of the points covered in chapter 2 can be applied to individuals as well as groups.

Let them know how often you will need their services and ask them to choose from a list of tasks that they can do. Remember to remind them of the benefits of participation. Some suggestions which produce likely sources of volunteers are: Friends of the Library, Retired Teachers Associations, Parent Organizations, Church Groups, Senior Citizens, Teen Groups, Business Partners, and civic groups. Remember also to write a press release for newsletters and the local papers about your search for volunteers.

WORKSHEET 6-1

VOLUNTEER RECRUITMENT FORM

Name: _____ **Address:** _____

Interview Date: _____ **Phone:** _____

Best Time To Call:

1. Why are you interested in volunteering for the library?

2. Have you ever worked with children before?
   What ages?   In what capacity?

3. What special skills do you have?
   - Speak a language other than English (which one(s)?) _____
   - Craft/artistic ability _____
   - Story telling _____
   - Puppet/theater _____
   - Other _____

4. What are some of your favorite children's books? (Do you have a library card?)

5. What is your availability?
   Days of the week: _____
   Time of the day: _____
   Do you have transportation? _____

6. Is there anything you would like to add that you feel is appropriate for us to know?

   Interviewed By: _____

WORKSHEET 6-2

VOLUNTEER COMMITMENT FORM

Name _____

Date _____

I am willing to commit _____ hours per _____ to the Main Street Public
Library's Outreach Program. I understand that I will attend an orientation session
about the program and will then receive an assignment. I further agree that I will
notify the library if a conflict in scheduling arises at least one week prior to the program, unless it is a case of extreme emergency. I understand that the library agrees
to provide the training and materials I will need for the program and will assume the
responsibility for scheduling all programs.

_____   _____

Librarian's Signature   **Volunteer's Signature**

ENDNOTES

1. Association for Library Service to Children. *Competencies for Librarians Serving Children in the Public Library*. 1991.

2. Virginia H. Mathews, et al. "Kids Need Libraries." In *School Library Journal*, 36:4 (April 1990):33-37.

7 BRIDGING THE GAP

To the outsider, library services for children and youth means just what it says: programs and services from birth through the teenage years. We would be doing children a great disservice, however, if we failed to recognize that our responsibility must also extend to all of the adult caregivers who work with children every day. This means a wide range of people: parents, grandparents, day care workers, and teachers. Their knowledge of the library and their needs may vary greatly. To foster relationships with these individuals, we need to get to know them and their needs, and address them accordingly. Nurturing these partnerships is a key step in the development and the success of outreach services. This chapter is intended to give you some insight into this area, and some assistance with bridging the gap.[1]

Given the necessity for outreach services, you will find many parents, guardians and caregivers who are not familiar with the library and its services. It will be up to you to both stimulate their sense of need for your services and to satisfy it. If our outreach services are going to be effective, we must accept the fact that the role that books play in a child's life directly depends upon the adults who are following up and reinforcing the brief exposure to reading enjoyment the library can offer.

REACHING TEACHERS

Teachers will most often consider you to be a resource person. They will come to you knowing that books are important. They will want to know specific titles to select and how to use these books with children in the learning program. They will want help in figuring out how to match a particular child or group of children with an appropriate book. They will want to observe your techniques so that they too can make books come alive for their children. Teachers are aware of the value of reading aloud, and will look to you to help them provide memorable and entertaining experiences.[2] Following is a suggested program outline.

TEACHERS IN-SERVICE PROGRAM

Program Purpose: To inform teachers of the materials and services that are available at the local library.

Program Background: The local public library has many items that can be helpful within the classroom. Even though support of the public school instructional program is not the primary mission of the public library, that is where your school-age clients spend much of their day, and the school library may not be adequate. The teachers may be unaware of your library's resources if they live out of town, are not familiar with the library, or have not used the children's library for a time. They may also be unaware of the library's limitations as well. Offer to help them find the materials they need and keep track of the results with a form such as the one in Figure 7-1.

Figure 7-1 Teacher Search Results Form

Main Street Public Library
105 Main Street, Anytown, Connecticut 06450
Phone: (203) 233-READ

A Librarian assisted search on:

> *Subject*

> *Author*

> *Title*

_____ Search did not supply needed information

_____ Circulating Material is checked out

_____ No other material is available at appropriate reading level

Both Children's and Reference Department appreciate advance knowledge of student library assignment.

IMPLEMENTATION PROCESS
1. Contact the school administration and ask to set up a time to discuss the In-service Proposal.

2. Meet with the appropriate authorities and discuss the need to have such a program. Present a draft outline of what should be covered.

3. Be prepared to present documentation of your credentials. Many states require that the proposal and your data be reviewed to qualify for continuing education credits.

4. Offer to hold the training at the library if you facility can handle this. This is good because you can show, as well as talk about, the library. However, it may not be possible in all cases.

5. Explain and policies or special services that may be available, as well as the library's overall services (see Figure 7-2). Make sure you are aware of the amount of time you have to speak, and plan accordingly.

6. Facilitate the process of getting library cards for all teachers and for any of their students who do not have one (see Figure 7-3).

Hints for a Successful Program

1. Careful panning: Know you audience, your materials, and the amount of time you have for a presentation. A typical presentation might proceed as follows:

   - Welcome introduction.
   - Tour of the facility.
   - Explanation of library services.
   - Special services available to teachers.
   - Importance of planning ahead and communicating needs to library in advance—examples.
   - Resources that may be helpful.
   - Library willingness to coperate.
   - Questions and answers.
   - Wrap-up.

2. Offer this to private and parochial schools as well as public schools.

Figure 7-2 Sample Letter to Teachers

Main Street Public Library
105 Main Street, Anytown, Connecticut 06450
Phone: (203) 233-READ

Dear Teacher:

Our Library Staff would like to welcome you back to another great year. We encourage you to make use of the Main Street Public Library for your classes. Teacher's collections have become an important and successful part of our children's library. We're very pleased to be able, once again, to offer this service.

The primary benefit of the teacher's card is to eliminate fines on classroom materials. Schools will be responsible, however, if the materials are not returned to the library after the end of the term, and they will be billed accordingly.

In order to facilitate your requests, we have devised a simple set of guidelines.

1. If you either live or teach in Anytown you may apply for a Teacher's Library Card. It is separate from your personal library card and will have a separate bar code. Expired cards should be brought to the circulation desk. If you are applying for a teacher's card for the first time, please bring one of the following forms of identification:

   a. Teacher Federation Card

   b. Recent Pay Stub

   c. Letter of introduction from your current school

   d. Your name listed in the Board of Education directory.

   Please be sure all information is current. Our circulation staff will be happy to correct any errors. You must bring this card with you when charging out a collection.

Figure 7-2 Sample Letter to Teachers (Cont.)

2. Requests should be dropped off at least one week before materials are needed.

3. The Children's Staff asks that you limit your collection as other teachers may need some of the same material. Staff reserves the right to limit high demand items.

4. Through experience we find that by the time reserved books and books from other libraries arrive at the desk, the materials are no longer needed. Consequently this service will no longer be available, except in emergencies.

5. Collections left beyond the specified pick-up date will be shelved.

6. Books charged out on Teacher's Collection Library Cards will be checked out in the Children's Library and returned to the main circulation desk.

7. You are responsible for all items charged on your Teacher's Card and will be billed accordingly for damaged or lost items.

Just as a reminder, the card is not to be used for any personal reading materials, and it is only valid at the Main Street Public Library.

Sincerely,

Marcia Trotta
Children's Librarian

3. Repeat often. It is better to do this in smaller groups so you meet the teachers personally and there is time for questions.

4. Be prepared to meet the demand! This program works to bring more people into the library.

Figure 7-3 Sample Letter to Teachers

Main Street Public Library
105 Main Street, Anytown, Connecticut 06450
Phone: (203) 233-READ

Dear Teachers:

We would like to invite you and your students to become card holders at the Main Street Public Library. For your convenience, we have provided applications in both English and Spanish. Please distribute them to the children and have them taken home to be filled out. Children under 7th grade are required to have the approval of a parent or guardian. When the forms are returned to school, we would appreciate your checking them over to see if a parent has indeed signed. Once they are collected, you can have them sent down to me at the library. Please mark the front of the batch with your name and grade so that we can deliver the cards to you.

Just a word about our teacher card -- this card can be used in addition to your regular library card. It offers you some special features: longer borrowing periods, no fines on overdues, and our staff will put together subject/special collections for you to pick up with a few days notice. Many teachers in the city are taking advantage of this opportunity.

We hope that we can be of service to you. Please call if you have any questions.

Sincerely,

Marcia Trotta
Director of Children's Services

SAMPLE BUDGET

Staff:

20 programs per year (requiring		
3 hours for presentation;		
3 hours for preparation): 120hrs @ 15/hr		$1,800.00
Flyers, applications, etc.		100.00
Refreshments		200.00
Total		**$2,100.00**

REACHING CARE GIVERS

Day care providers, especially home centered ones, are often surprised that library services are available to them! This attitude stems from the fact that these are businesses. Another factor that comes into play is the wide diversity of experience among the providers. Our responsibility is to alert them to what we are doing, and to offer cooperative programs. A model program for launching services was done in Guilford, Connecticut. Lana Ferguson and Sue Ellen Croteau developed an extensive annotated bibliography of materials appropriate to use in most day care situations. Funded by an LSCA grant, they published *Building Blocks* and held open houses to which they invited all local day care providers for its distribution and for the promotion of other library services.[3]

Parents and grandparents also need to become aware of the range of library services available to the children in their care as well as programs that will help them become better caregivers. In recent years, national attention has been focused on the increasingly serious problem of adult illiteracy—a major factor affecting off-site services. Parents are their child's first teacher. If they are not functionally literate chances are quite high that they will pass a reading disability on to another generation. Outreach programming with a family literacy approach is a solution. It gives us the opportunity to break the cycle of illiteracy that underlies a vast array of social and economic problems. The library's role in providing programs for parents is thus of utmost importance. A great deal of current research documents the fact that children who are read to learn to read more easily, earlier in life, and maintain that head start throughout their school career. It has also been shown that seeing parents reading for their own information and enjoyment provides one key impetus for children to become readers. Claudia Jones states "There is a world of difference in the child whose parents are actively involved in his learning and children who are left on their own—not only in ability, but in quality of work, attitude and self-image."[4]

Parents who become involved in their children's education early on are apt to stay involved throughout their schooling. Effective parent programs may be the catalyst that some parents need. Your goal with parents is to get them to take a real part in the program. They have a natural inclination to want the best for their child. There are many ways to involve them in the process if you are creative, and if you plan programs in locations that are congenial and welcoming to this group.

What kinds of programs are suitable for parents? There is no one answer. You will want to tailor offerings based on needs you observe in your community. Some ideas include how to select books to read aloud; good nutrition habits; communication; discipline. We all learn to be parents through trial and error. Simply bringing parents together with others who are experiencing feelings of doubt is a *terrific* program. Another possibility is creating a liaison between parents and people in social service, health, or other community agencies who can help them. Whatever works is great—just keep the atmosphere non-critical, non-threatening and non-judgmental!

PARENT PROGRAM: HELPING CHILDREN READ

Ideas To Share With Parents

Infants: Mother Goose Rhymes, songs, easy poetry. Let them listen to the sounds of your voice, and the rhymes of the words. Objectives:

- Developing effective listening skills. Infants begin to recognize the variations of voice tones and expressions. The infant learns to associate books with place and security.
- Parents learn that it is never too early to begin reading to their child. They learn what materials are appropriate to use.
- Provides an opportunity for bonding between parent and child.

Toddlers: Concept books, books of animals, books with familiar objects and sounds. Objectives:

- Children begin to repeat sounds. They are able to recognize similarities and differences.
- Enjoyable, participatory sessions for parents and children.
- Beginning vocabulary development. Parents learn that children will learn to read as they learned to speak, by repeating what they hear.

Preschoolers: Stories, fingerplays, puzzles or other realia. Objectives:

- Literature is a means of exploring emotions and feelings and how to deal with them. Children are more able to accept themselves if they see other children in similar situations.
- Development of hand-eye coordination (necessary to read).
- Concentration and memorization skills are built by using other formats.
- Encouraging parents to use other materials to supplement books.

These are examples of some of the sessions that you could provide for parents. They may not be aware that there are certain skills that a child must develop in order to become a reader. You might also provide parents with these simple guidelines:

HOW TO ENCOURAGE READING

1. Read every day—this encourages children to want to read.
2. Play with them every day—shapes, colors and concepts through puzzles, toys, and games—this builds pre-letter readiness.
3. Talk to children and ask them to tell you stories. Write them down. This develops imagination, and an understanding of sequencing.

4. Have many items available. Buy them if you can, remember to borrow them from the library, but have a variety around.

5. Recipe for nourishing a lifelong treasure of delight:

Take 1 relaxed child
1 book of any variety
1 accommodating lap
Combine with a person who enjoys a book and shows it.
Take enough time, and serve daily—*Anonymous*

6. Use story extenders to reinforce the learning experience. For example, read Eric Carle's *The Very Hungry Caterpillar*. Show children real caterpillars and butterflies or Shaw's It *Looked Like Spilt Milk* and have deep blue paper, cotton balls and glue so the children can create their own (cloud) pictures.

7. Ask questions about the text. Comprehension skills are built when the answers to questions are found.

8. Make learning to read easy, enjoyable, and a frequent experience.

Using items like these helps parents become comfortable and confident that they *can* make a powerful impact on their child's reading. They are the means of bridging the gap!

You may have tangible wealth untold,
Caskets of jewels and coffers of gold.
Richer than I you can never be—
I had a mother who read to me.[5]

PARENT SUPPORT COALITION

Program Purpose: To provide parents with the opportunity to receive support and assistance in raising their children.

Program Background: It is no secret that while we receive education for many things, very few of us receive training on how to parent. This program is designed to provide much needed guidance and support to parents who are struggling to raise healthy, well-adjusted children. In addition, it has the potential of developing a peer network for the participants. Materials

Required: Expert resource people, library books, supportive staff, promotional materials, refreshments.

IMPLEMENTATION STEPS

1. Do some preparation work to determine if there is a need for this parent program in the community, and what days and times are most convenient.

2. Meet with the heads of town departments that may have the expert staff necessary to develop this program. This might be the Department of Health or the Department of Children and Youth Services.

3. Make connections with other agencies in the community which could also be of assistance in organizing this program and providing speakers.

4. Develop an agenda of topics that could be covered in this parenting series. Suggestions: Communications, Discipline, Encouraging Positive Behavior, Developing Self-Esteem, Nutrition, Health Care Alerts.

5. If funding is required, involve a business or civic organization to help underwrite it.

6. Advertise the series. It is helpful to have parents register so that you have an idea of how many are going to attend.

7. You might want to consider working with a group that will be able to provide babysitting services for the parents at low or no cost so they can attend the workshop. Friends of the Library might be a source to tap; or a local day care center.

8. Prepare lists of library materials that provide additional information on each of the topics. Do a book display at each of the events. Also have refreshments available.

9. Do a short introduction to the programs about the library and its services. Welcome parents and tell them you will be around to answer their questions after the program is over.

10. Write thank you notes to all appropriate parties.

HINTS FOR A SUCCESSFUL PROGRAM

1. Remember to promote the library as a resource and one solution to many of our social problems.
2. Check the speakers' references. If at all possible, try to sit in on one of their presentations elsewhere.
3. Make sure that the parents who leave their children with the babysitting service feel confident that their children are in good hands.
4. Keep the programs to a reasonable length—no more than one-and-a-half hours is appropriate.

SAMPLE BUDGET

Speakers:	4 for Series @ $100/ea.	$400.00
Promotional materials		25.00
Refreshments 50.00		
Misc. materials		25.00
Total		**$500.00**

PARENTSHARE ANNOUNCEMENT

Come and join this series of informative discussions designed to help us in our jobs as parents.

October 1: 6:30 p.m.	**Talk with Me:** Communication Strategies
October 8: 6:30 p.m.	**Healthy Treats:** Ruth Fields, R.D.; Discussion Leader
October 15: 6:30 p.m.	**Correct Me if I'm Wrong:** Discipline that works Joseph Jones, Ph.D.; Discussion Leader
October 22: 6:30 p.m.	**Health Alerts:** Terry Treble, M.D.; Discussion Leader

Programs will last approximately one-and-a-half hours.

Childcare is available. Refreshments will be served.

Call 333-1203 to register: Main Street Public Library, 803 Main Street

Co-sponsored by the Children's Coalition.

PARENT COMMITMENTS:

- Treat children with love and respect.
- Give your child space to grow, to dream, to succeed, and to fail.
- Let your child be him- or herself, not who you want him or her to be.
- When you discipline, let your children know that you disapprove of what they did, not who they are.
- Set limits for your children, and let them know what is expected of them.
- Make time for your child and realize how important that time is.
- Encourage the child to experience as much as he or she can.
- Be a positive model for your child—fair, moral, loving, and giving.

You may be feeling somewhat overwhelmed and perhaps not qualified to take on parenting programs, but you must remember how important they are to the overall success of your mission. Also remember that you do not have to present all the programs yourself! Look to your alliances and coalitions! You have a wealth of talent among the allies you have won within your community and they will often present a program if asked. Remember the library is the information place! Whatever approach you choose, you will be helping individuals develop their capabilities so they can help their children's development. In supporting parents with these positive efforts, you are providing a means for your outreach efforts to carry over into the home environment. You may also be able to connect parents to the program by using their individual talents and cultural backgrounds as resources. They may even become volunteers. This is another way to develop continuity between the program and home.

THE LEARNING ENVIRONMENT

A vital part of predisposing a child toward reading is creating a *learning environment*. Children become literate when they are personally involved with significant adults who take reading seriously. Worksheet 7-1 is an easy checklist that parents, day care workers, and others can use to determine whether they are creating an atmosphere that encourages reading. Remember the importance of adult modeling: setting a good example by letting children see that you are reading for yourself is of great value. Children learn to read naturally when they are surrounded by people who love to read, who read to them, and who respond to reading to others with enthusiasm. Children who do not have this are not being encouraged to develop lifetime reading habits, and they will be at a disadvantage all of their lives.

WORKSHEET 7-1

LEARNING ENVIRONMENT CHECKLIST

1. What Do I Read?

Item: Titles:

Newspaper _____

Magazine _____

Books _____

2. How often do I read? Number of hours:

Daily _____

Weekly _____

Monthly_____

3. Why Do I Read?

_____ To explore that part of my mind and spirit that is buried under the daily grind.

_____ To get information and current news.

_____ To learn new things and expand my horizons.

_____ For pleasure and escape from worries and problems.

4. What do I enjoy about reading?

5. Where do I get my reading materials?

_____ Buy at store

_____ Come in mail

_____ From the library

6. Where do I keep/store my reading materials?

RESOURCES

BOOKS FOR PARENTS

Andrew, J. *Divorce and the American Family*. New York: Watts, 1978.

Atlas, S. L. *Single Parenting: A Practical Resource Guide*. Englewood Cliffs, NJ: Prentice-Hall, 1981.

Bosco, A. *Successful Single Parenting*. Mystic, CT: Twenty-third, 1978.

Craine, L. *Widow*. New York: Bantam, 1975.

Galper, M. *Joint Custody and Co-parenting: Sharing Your Child Equally—A Source Book for the Separated or Divorced Family*. Philadelphia: Running Press, 1980.

Hope, K. and Young, N. *Momma Handbook: The Source Book for Single Mothers*. New York: New American Library, 1976.

Jackson, M. and Jackson, J. *"Your Father's Not Coming Home Anymore."* New York: Richard Marek, 1981.

Klein, C. *The Single Parent Experience*. New York: Avon Books, 1978.

Pincus, L. *Death and the Family*. New York: Random, 1976.

Reed, B. *I Didn't Plan to Be a Single Parent!* St. Louis, MO: Condordia, 1981.

Rowlands, P. *Saturday Parent: A Book for Separated Families*. New York: Continuum, 1982.

Salk, L. *What Every Child Would Like Parents to Know about Divorce*. New York: Warner Books, 1979.

Turow, R. *Daddy Doesn't Live Here Anymore*. Garden City, NY: Anchor Books, 1978.

BOOKS FOR CHILDREN: FICTION

Alexander, A. *To Live a Lie*. (Ages 8-12) New York: Antheneum, 1975.

Blume, J. *It's Not the End of the World*. (Ages 9-12) Scarsdale, NY: Bradbury Press, 1972.

Girion, B. *A Tangle of Roots*. (Ages 12 and up) New York: Scribner, 1979.

Goff, B. *Where is Daddy?* (Ages 4-8) New York: Beacon, 1969.

Hunt, I. *William*. (Ages 10 and up) New York: Ace, 1981.

Le Shan, E. *What's Going to Happen to Me?* (Ages 8 and up) Bristol, FL: Four Winds, 1978.

Lexau, J. M. *Emily and the Klunky Baby and the Next Door Dog*. (Ages 4-8) New York: Dial Press, 1972.

Lexau, J. M. *Me Day*. (Ages 7-10) New York: Dial Press, 1972.

Mann, P. *My Dad Lives in a Downtown Hotel*. (Ages 9-11) New York: Doubleday, 1973.

Sallis, S. *An Open Mind*. (Ages 12 and up) New York: Harper and Row Publishers, 1978.

Sinberg, S. *Divorce Is a Grown-up Problem*. (Ages 4-6) New York: Avon Books, 1978.

Tax, M. *Families*. (Ages 3-6) Boston: Little, Brown, & Co., 1981.

Zolotow, C. *A Father Like That*. (Ages 4-7) New York: Harper & Row Publishers, 1971.

BOOKS FOR CHILDREN: NONFICTION

Berger, T. *How Does it Feel when Your Parents Get Divorced?* (Ages 6-11) New York: Messner, 1977.

Casey, J. *"What's a Divorce Anyway?"* (Ages 6-10) New York: Vantage, 1981.

Fayerweather Street School. E. Rofes, ed. *The Kids Book of Divorce*. (Ages 7 and up) Lexington, MA: Lewis Publishing Co., 1981.

Gardner, R.A. *The Boys and Girls Book about Divorce*. (Ages 7-14) New York: Bantam Books, 1970.

Gardner, R.A. *The Boys and Girls Book about One Parent Families*. (Ages 7-14) New York: Putnam Publishing Group, 1978.

Krementz, J. *How It Feels When a Parent Dies*. (All ages) New York: Knopf, 1981.

List, J. A. *The Day the Loving Stopped*. New York: Fawcett, 1981. All ages.

Pursell, M. S. *A Look at Divorce*. (Ages 3-7) Minneapolis, MN: Lerner Publications, 1976.

Richards, A. and Willis, I. *How to Get It Together When Your Parents Are coming Apart*. (Ages 7 and up) New York: McKay, 1976.

ADDITIONAL RESOURCES

The following books contain additional bibliographics and information about written and audiovisual materials for children.

Bernstein, J. E. *Books to Help Children Cope with Separation and Loss. Second Ed.*. New York: Bowker, 1983.

Dreyer, S. S. *Bookfinder: A Guide to Children's Literature about the Needs and Problems of Youth—Aged 2-15*. Circle Pine, MN: American Guidance Service, Inc., 1981.

Horner, C. T. *The Single Parent Family in Children's Books*. Metuchen, NJ: Scarecrow Press, Inc., 1978.

ENDNOTES

1. Claudia Jones, *Parents are Teachers Too* (Charlotte, VT: Williamson Publishing Co., 1988), 11.

2. Neil Colburn, "Choosing and Using Books for the Youngest Children," in *First Steps to Literacy* (Chicago: American Library Association, 1990), 1.

3. Lana Ferguson and Sue Ellen Croteau, *Building Blocks: An Annotated Bibliography for Day Care Providers Serving Children Ages 2 through 5* (Guilford, CT: Guilford Free Library, 1992).

4. Jones, Op. Cit., 47.

5. Strickland Sullivan, "Reading Mother," in *Best Loved Poems of the American People*, Hazel Felleman, ed. (New York: Doubleday, 1936).

8 PROMOTING OUTREACH SERVICES

NEW TWISTS TO REACH YOUR AUDIENCE

Promotion of outreach services requires a two-pronged approach, because, in most instances, you will be trying to reach two different audiences. The first audience is composed of groups who will support the program. You may be looking to gain community goodwill or recognition from them *and* you may be looking for their financial support. Once you have decided what it is you need, and with whom you would like to talk, you can develop a traditional promotional campaign. This may include news releases, solicitation letters, information talks to civic groups, items in the Friends newsletter, etc. Very often, this level of promotion begins *before* you start on the implementation of outreach services. Updates are then provided once services are established.

The second audience is your targeted clientele. The promotion you develop to reach them may include some of the usual strategies that the library uses for its other services. Radio Public Service Announcements (PSAs), press releases in the newspaper, posters and flyers may all be appropriate. You must be aware that your target population of non-users may not be reached by these methods, and you will need to observe their habits carefully if your promotional efforts are to be effective. If you have feedback that a group doesn't read or understand English, then you will want to develop materials in all languages that are appropriate. If you find that there is difficulty in reading, you will want to take advantage of audiovisual resources. Your print materials must then be mostly pictorial. In all instances, the materials should be crisp, attractive and to the point. A representative assortment of materials is shown in Figure 8-1 through 8-13 at the end of this chapter.

GETTING STARTED: AREAS TO CONSIDER

Refer to your list of other agencies in town that serve children and families. Ask them to display posters, distribute flyers, and include information about your program in their newsletters.

Suggestions:
- Community Action Groups
- Head Start Centers

- Day Care Centers
- Nursery Schools
- Hospitals/Clinics
- Parks, Recreational Facilities
- Housing Complexes

Look for Bulletin Boards in Community Locations. Get permission to put up attractive displays. (If you or your staff are not artistic, ask for help from the art department of a local high school or college, or look for volunteers.)

Suggestions:
- Supermarkets
- Banks
- Department Stores

Arrange to speak to local groups that have some interest in children.

Suggestions:
- Civic Groups
- Church Groups
- Parent Groups
- Housing Associations

Arrange to piggy-back on advertising by local businesses. This is often quite possible in print formats like placemats at a fast food restaurant or posters on a bus. Again audio and visual presentations (commercials on local radio and television) can be quite effective.

Develop information packets that can be distributed throughout the community. These should be given in quantities to homeless shelters, battered women's shelters, clinics, doctors, dentists. Get their support in distributing them and their input on the contents.

Make visits everywhere in the community where you will find children, parents, and families.

Suggestions:
- Parks
- Recreational Facilities
- YWCA/YMCA

Use photos—in newspapers, in store windows, etc. They really are worth 1,000 words! They can be especially helpful to people who do not read!

There are many other ideas that work. Be creative and innovative. And remember that the most effective promotion of all is word of mouth. By providing good service and quality programs, you will enlist the participants of previous programs as promoters. They can become your most effective tool.

It is often easier to promote a series than a single event. If you promote several dates ahead of time, people can choose which programs to attend or plan for all of them. Make dates, times, and locations very visible.

Figure 8-1 Sample News Item for Bulletins

LIBRARY NAME

Contact Person:
Phone:

A family story hour will be held every Saturday at the Main Street Pavilion. The program will run from 10:00 a.m. to 11:00 a.m. All are welcome. Call the library at 202-9031 for details.

SAMPLE RADIO ANNOUNCEMENT

Feed your children's minds as well as their bodies! Come to the McDonald's play yard on Saturday, June 20 from 11:00 a.m. to 12:00 noon. The Children's Library staff will treat the whole family to delicious stories. The program is free and is sponsored by McDonald's and the City Library.

Figure 8-2 Sample Newsletter Article

The Main Street Public Library is joining forces with the YWCA Day Camp this summer to bring children great vacation reading.

Janie Lee, Director of Children's Library and a staff of enthusiastic volunteers will be reading to children every morning. Their book selections will be on summertime themes. For older children, book discussion groups will be held.

The purpose of the program is to encourage children to read on their own for pleasure as well as information. Children will be encouraged to get library cards and select materials from the library's bookmobile which will be available.

As an added feature, a "drawing" will be held daily. The prize books have been donated by Mr. Chris Rule of Rule's Book World.

Anyone interested in assisting the library with this program is asked to call Ms. Lee at 737-2207.

Figure 8-3

Information About the Library—Spanish / English

More than Books

MATERIALS AND SERVICES
OF THE
CHILDREN'S LIBRARY

105 Main Street, Anytown, USA

233-READ

Library Hours

Monday-Thursday	10 a.m. - 8 p.m.
Friday	10 a.m. - 5 p.m.
Saturday	9 a.m. - 5 p.m.
Sunday	1 p.m. - 5 p.m.

FOR PARENTS AND TEACHERS:

1. Parents' shelf: Special materials to aid in the tough job of raising children.

2. Parent Workshops: Special programs with qualified guest speakers about childrearing issues.

3. Teachers Collection: The staff will assist teachers in gathering materials for their class. Ask for details.

4. Tours and group visits for class and scout troops are available (reservations required).

Mucho mas que Libros

SERVICIOS Y MATERIALES
DE LA
BIBLIOTECA DE NINOS

105 Main Street Anytown, USA

233-READ

PARA PADRES Y MAESTROS:

1. Area de Padres: Coleccion de informacion que le ayudaran en la tarea dificil de criar ninos.

2. Orientacion para Padres: Programas especiales con oradores calificados para presentar temas sobre la crianza de los hijos.

3. Coleccion para Maestros: Los maestros pueden obtener assistencia para reunir materiales e informacion para sus clases, pida mas detalles.

4. Obtenga Informacion sobre giras y visitas para estudiantes y otros grupos. Se requiere reservacion.

Horas de

la Biblioteca

Lunes - Jueves	10 a.m. - 8 p.m.
Viernes	10 a.m. - 5 p.m.
Sabado	9 a.m. - 5 p.m.
Domingo (Noviembre - Abril)	1 p.m. - 4 p.m.

Figure 8-4 English Language Promotional Flyer

THE CHILDREN'S LIBRARY

has many resources to offer in addition to its outstanding

book collection!

Information Services: Call or come in and our librarians will help you answer questions. No, we don't do HOME-WORK! We will help you find materials to do it yourself.

Programs: A variety of programs is offered for children of all ages. Ask for the current newsletter for coming attractions.

Toys to Go: We have an exciting variety of toys that may be borrowed for use at home.

Posters: Does your room need a change? Framed posters are available for your use.

Foreign Languages: Would you like to learn a new language? Our records, tapes, and books will make it fun.

Records and Cassettes: Hear some stories, songs, or music to help you practice dance steps. Cassettes are very handy for car trips.

Vertical File: Check out our pamphlet file for current information, especially good for school reports.

Magazines: We have the very best on the market! Check some out today.

Large Type: Books are available with enlarged print that makes reading easy on the eyes.

I Can Read: Books with larger print and a controlled vocabulary to encourage new readers.

Videotapes: A large selection of educational and entertaining videotapes suitable for a child's viewing are here for parents to make their selections.

Figure 8-5: Spanish Language Promotional Flyer

LA BIBLIOTECA DE LOS NINOS

Tiene otros medios disponibles para disfrutar de la

biblioteca ademas de los libros!

Servicios Informativos: Llame o venga a la biblioteca y nuestros bibliotecarios le contestaran sus preguntas. No haran tu tarea pero te ayudaran con los materiales que necesitas.

Programas: Ofrecemos una gran variedad de programas para ninos de todas las edades. Pida un calendario de los eventos para las proximas semanas.

Juguetes: Tenemos una excitante variedad de juguetes que pueden cojer prestados para usar en su hogar.

Carteles: Quieres decorar una habitacion? Tenemos carteles montados que puedes usar.

Lenguaje Extranjero: Deseas aprender una lengua nueva? Nuestros discos, casetes y libros te ayudaran.

Discos y Casetes: Escuche cuentos grabados, canciones y musica para bailar. Los casetes son buenos para escuchar especialmente cuando vas de viaje.

Archivo Vertical: Folletos con informacion util para hacer reportajes escolares.

Revistas: Tenemos lo mejor en el mercado, llevese varios.

Imprenta Grande: Libros de imprenta grande para facilitar la lectura.

Yo Puedo Leer: Una serie de libros con las letras grandes para estimular a los nuevos lectores.

Videos: Una gran seleccion de videos educacional y de entretenimiento apropriado para ninos, los padres haran la seleccion.

Figure 8-6

FAMILY READING CLUB

The Family Read-Aloud Club is designed to encourage families to develop the habit of reading aloud together. Studies have shown that reading aloud makes a difference. Children who are read aloud to are more successful in school. The emphasis is on a regular time set aside for reading as a family, not on the number of books read.

1. The family makes a contract agreeing to read a certain number of minutes each day for 28 days. It is the family's decision what the daily reading goal will be. There is a minimum goal of ten minutes, but the family may choose a longer time for a daily goal. Every family who participates may have a picture taken for the "Family Reading Hall of Fame." Pictures may be picked up in March after the club ends.

2. Each day the family completes the reading goal, one heart on the reading record sheet is colored in. There are more days to the club than there are hearts, so if you register early you can afford to miss a day occasionally.

3. Only one heart is marked off per day, even if you spend more time reading.

4. When you have completed 28 days of reading, hand in your game sheet. We will return it to you with your prize and certificate at the party on March 27. If you finish early, please hand it in early. Your completed reading game sheet must be turned in by 5:00 p.m., March 15!

5. Prizes and certificates will be awarded at the Awards Party on March 27 at 3:45 p.m. If you plan to attend, please sign up to bring a food item to share. If you cannot attend, you can pick up your prize and certificate at the library after March 27.

6. You may use any reading material you wish. It doesn't have to be library books. Any adult connected to your family, such as a grandparent or sitter may read to the children. An older child may read to a younger one on occasion. Children may be read to at different times during the day, but each one should be read to for the contract time.

Have Fun!!!

Figure 8-7

Family Read-Aloud Club Contract

Our family understands the value of reading aloud, and we wish to participate in the Family Read-Aloud Club. Our goal is for someone in our family to read aloud to:

_____

(Names of Children)

at least _____ minutes a day for 28 days.

_____   _____

(Parent's signature)   (Date)

Figure 8-8

CERTIFICATE OF READING AWARD

This certificate is awarded to _____ for being an active and enthusiastic reader. You have realized that books are an important, fun, and exciting part of everyday life.

Signed,

_____

Main Street Public Library

Figure 8-9 This Can Be a Poster or Flyer

Parent Share

Being a parent is hard work! Join other parents and Jan Biodie, staff counselor, in these informative get-togethers.

March 15	**Communication and Cooperation**
March 22	**Raising Responsible Kids**
March 29	**Discipline That Works**
April 5	**Love You Forever**

All programs are being held in the reception room at the clinic from 10:30 a.m. until noon. Story and activities are planned for children at the same time.

The program is offered to you free and is sponsored by the Main Street Public Library and the Visiting Nurses Association. Call 233-READ for information.

Figure 8-10 Sample Flyer

Flyers to display or pass out at community sites

Parenting Plus

Parents: Visit the Main Street Public Library!

FOR KIDS!

There are:
Picture story books
Board books
Concept books
Toys
Puzzles
Shape sorters
Games
Records
Cassettes
Videos

FOR YOU!

Books on baby and child care
Magazines on parenting topics
Videos by *Parents' Magazine*:
"Meeting the World"
"Learning About the World"
"Postnatal Exercises"
"Baby Safe Home"

All of this and more can be borrowed free from the Main Street Public Library 105 Main Street 233-READ.

Figure 8-11 Sample Flyer

Help someone become a reader! Replace a paperback book with a hardcover book. We will see that a child who needs a book receives it during the HOLIDAY SEASON. Share the gift of reading! Donations accepted during our library's open hours.

Main Street Public Library
Children's Department
105 Main Street
Anytown, USA 06444
233-READ

Figure 8-12 This Can Be a Poster or Flyer

Grandparents' Day

Story Hour

Monday, September 11

4:30 p.m.

Senior Center Program Room

Attention Grandparents! Bring your grandchild to this special story hour in your honor. We will be reading some stories and doing some activities in celebration of the day. There is no age requirement, but we'd like to know how many will be attending, so please register in advance! Sponsored by the Main Street Public Library and the WP Senior Center.

Call 233-READ for details!

Figure 8-13 Sample Flyer

Stories for Children

by

Main Street Public Library

at

W.I.C.

Program Free   All Welcome

Monday, June 11

8:30 a.m. - 4:00 p.m.

Call 233-READ for more information

Cuentos Para Ninos

por

La Biblioteca Publica de Anytown, USA

en

W.I.C.

El Programa es Gratis Todos son bienvenidos

El lunes 11 de Junio

8:30 a.m. - 4:00 p.m.

Para mas informacion llame al 238-READ

RESOURCES

BUS SAFETY

Barbato, Juli. *From Bed To Bus*.

Cole, Joanna. *The Magic School Bus At The Water Works*.

———. *The Magic School Bus: Inside The Earth*.

Crews, Donald. *School Bus*.

Gackenbach, Dick. *What's Claude Doing?*

Haywood, Carolyn. *Here Comes The Bus!*

Nichols, Paul. *Big Paul's School Bus*

BICYCLE SAFETY

Breinburg, Petronella. *Shawn's Red Bike*.

Rey, H.A. *Curious George Rides a Bike*.

Silver, Rosalie. *David's First Bicycle*.

Coombs, Richard. *Bicycling*.

Fink, Joanne. *Things to Know Before Buying a Bicycle*.

Kessler, Leonard. *A Tale of Two Bicycles*.

Lawler, Tony. *Beginner's Guide to Bicycling and Bike Maintenance*.

BACK TO SCHOOL

A Booklist prepared by the Staff of the Main Street Public Library to assist children with their schoolwork, and to enjoy the school adventures of some of the best fiction characters.

Berry, Marilyn. *Help is on the Way for Reading Skills*.

———. *What to Do when your Mom and Dad Say . . . Do Your Homework*.

Christopher, Matt. *That Basket Counts.*

Conford, Ellen. *Anything for a Friend.*

Gallagher, Nora. *How to Stop a Sentence and Other Methods of Managing Words.*

Greene, Constance. *A Girl Called Al.*

Greenwald, Sheila. *Alvin Webster's Surefire Plan for Success (and How it Failed).*

Haywood, Carolyn. *Growing Up with Science.*

Hurwitz, Johanna. *Rip Roaring Russell.*

Jones, Rebeca. *Germy Blew It!*

Kyte, Kathy. *In Charge: A Complete Handbook for Kids With Working Parents.*

Leiner, Katherine. *Both My Parents Work.*

Lowry, Lois. *Rabble Starky.*

Marsoli, Lisa. *Things To Know About Babysitting.*

Peck, Richard. *Remembering the Good Times.*

Stanek, Muriel. *All Alone After School.*

Tolles, Martha. *Who's Reading Darci's Diary?*

Van Leeuween, Jean. *Benjy and the Power of Zingies.*

LET'S START SCHOOL
A Booklist prepared by the Staff of the Main Street Public Library for children beginning school.

Calmenso, Stephanie. *Kindergarten Book.*

Civardi, Anne. *Going To School.*

Cohen, Miriam. *Will I Have A Friend?*

Crews, Donald. *School Bus.*

Davis, Gibbs. *Katy's First Haircut.*

Delton, Judy. *The New Girl at School.*

Giff, Patricia. *Happy Birthday, Ronald Morgan!*

Howe, James. *When You Go To Kindergarten.*

Jenkins, Karen. *Kinder-Krunchies.*

Lindgren, Astrid. *I Want To Go To School.*

Mannhelm, Cerete. *The Two Friends.*

Nichols, Paul. *Big Paul's School Bus.*

Oxenbury, Helen. *First Day of School.*

Rinkoff, Barbara. *Rutherford T Finds 21 B.*

Ryan, Bernard. *How to Help Your Child Start School.*

Schwartz, Amy. *Annabelle Swift, Kindergartener.*

Schweninger, Ann. *Off to School.*

Sellers, Ronnie. *My First Day of School.*

Stein, Sara. *A Child Goes To School.*

9 RESOURCE DIRECTORY

There are many appropriate materials to use with outreach activities. The following items have been used successfully; however, it is most important for librarians to make those choices appropriate to their specific targeted audience. This requires that you develop and keep current a broad repertoire of materials from which to make your selections. A word of advice: include your favorites, but also pay special attention to multicultural materials, stories that deal with particular interests and issues, and books that deal with special needs. *Always* take the steps necessary to know your audience, and with children, make sure that the materials you choose are age-appropriate.

RESOURCES FOR CHILDREN

BOOKS

Ahlberg, Janet and Alan Ahlberg. *Each Peach Pear Plum*. Viking, 1979.

Aliki, illus. *Hush Little Baby: A Folk Lullabye*. Prentice-Hall, 1968.

Asch, Frank. *Sandcake*. Parents' Magazine Press, 1978.

Bang, Molly. *Ten, Nine, Eight*. Greenwillow, 1983.

Bridwell, Norman. *Clifford the Big Red Dog*. Scholastic, 1985.

Brown, Margaret Wise. *Goodnight Moon*. Harper, 1949.

Brown, Margaret Wise. *Runaway Bunny*. Harper, 1972

Bunting, Eve. *The Wednesday Surprise*. Clarion, 1989.

Campbell, Rod. *Dear Zoo*. Macmillan, 1984.

Carle, Eric. *The Very Hungry Caterpillar*. Putnam, 1981.

Carlstrom, Nancy White. *Jesse Bear, What Will You Wear?* Macmillan, 1986.

Clifton, Lucille. *Everett Anderson's Year*. Holt, 1974.

Crews, Donald. *Freight Train*. Greenwillow, 1978.

Degan, Bruce. *Jamberry*. Harper, 1983.

De Paola, Tomie. *Tomie de Paola's Mother Goose*. Putnam, 1985.

Ets, Marie Hall. *Gilberto and the Wind*. Viking, 1963.

Freeman, Don. *Corduroy*. Viking, 1968.

———. *A Rainbow of My Own*. Viking, 1966.

Galtone, Paul. *Gingerbread Boy*. Seabury, 1975.

———. *Three Little Kittens*. Clarion, 1986.

Gretz, Susanna. *Teddy Bears Go Shopping*. Four Winds, 1982.

Ginsburg, Maria. *Good Morning Chick*. Greenwillow, 1980.

Hill, Eric. *Where's Spot?* Putnam, 1987.

Hutchkins, Pat. *The Doorbell Rang*. Morrow, 1986.

———. *Titch*. Macmillan, 1982.

Jonas, Ann. *We Can Go*. Greenwillow, 1986.

Kalan, Robert. *Rain*. Greenwillow, 1978.

Keats, Ezra Jack. *Whistle for Willie*. Viking, 1964.

Kennedy, James. *Teddy Bear's Picnic*. Bedrick, 1987.

Kraus, Robert. *Leo the Late Bloomer*. Simon and Schuster, 1971

———. *Whose Mouse Are You?* Macmillan, 1970.

Lionni, Leo. *Swimmy*. Pantheon, 1966.

Lobel, Arnold. *Days with Frog and Toad*. Harper and Row, 1978.

McCloskey, Robert. *Make Way for Ducklings*. Viking, 1941.

Mack, Stan. *Ten Bears in My Bed*. Pantheon, 1974.

Mosel, Arlene. *Tikki Tembo*. Holt, 1968.

Omerod, Jan. *Moonlight*. Lothrop, 1982.

Oxenbury, Helen. *Tom and Peppo Read a Story*. Macmillan, 1988.

Poluskin, Maria. *Mother, Mother I Want Another*. Crown, 1978.

———.*Who Said Meow*? Crown, 1975.

Rae, Ellen. *All I Am*. Bradbury, 1990.

Rice, Eve. *Benny Bakes a Cake*. Greenwillow, 1981.

Rockwell, Anne F. *Three Bears and Fifteen other Stories*. Harper, 1975.

Schwartz, Amy. *Bea and Mr. Jones*. Bradbury, 1982.

Shaw, Charles. *It Looked Like Spilt Milk*. Harper, 1978.

Slobkina, Espher. *Cops for Sale*. Addison-Wesley, 1947.

Sendak, Maurice. *Chicken Soup with Rice*. Harper and Row, 1962.

Tafuri, Nancy. *Have You Seen My Duckling*? Greenwillow, 1984.

Wells, Rosemary. *Noisy Nora*. Dial, 1973.

Wildsmith, Brian. *Brian Wildsmith's 1, 2, 3*. Watts, 1965.

Zion, Gene. *Harry the Dirty Dog*. Harper, 1956.

SONGS AND FINGER-PLAYS

Brown, Marc. *Hand Rhymes*. Dutton, 1985.

Glazer, Tom. *Eyewinker, Tom Tinker, Chin Chopper: Fifty Musical Finger-plays*. Doubleday, 1973.

Grayson, Marion. *Let's Do Fingerplays*. Luce, 1962.

Kirchner, A.B. *Basic Beginners: A Handbook of Learning Games and Activities for Young Children.* New York: Acropolis, 1985.

Larrick, Nancy. *Wheels of the Bus Go Round and Round.* Golden Gate, 1972.

Longstaff, John. *Oh A-Hunting We Will Go.* Atheneum, 1983.

NONPRINT

Nonprint media are most helpful in doing outreach services. Due to the saturation of our lives with media and media products, they are a familiar and readily acceptable way to break the ice with individuals who are not accustomed to using library services. These products provide a non-threatening introduction to literature and library services, and the informal nature of this approach is an added benefit. Another less obvious but tremendous benefit that audiovisual products offer is that they broaden the staff's ability to work with people whose first language is not English. Recorded stories and songs that are of high quality employ readers and singers who are fluent in the language. Paying attention to this small detail is extremely important to the non-users. It gives them the perception that the library is being sensitive to them and that really gets you over the first hurdle. Following is a list of reliable companies that provide quality productions of useful nonprint media.

Records/Cassettes

Better Books Company
Department 874
P.O. Box 9770
Fort Worth, TX 76147-2770
1-800-433-5534

Caedmeon
HarperCollins
10 East 53rd Street
New York, NY 10022-5299
212-207-7000

Children's Literature in Audiovisual Media
Weston Woods
Weston, CT 06883-1199
1-800-243-5020

Listening Library Media Service
One Park Avenue
Old Greenwich, CT 06870-1727
1-800-243-4504

Spoken Arts
10100 S.B.F. Drive
Pinellas Park, FL 34666

Puppets and Other Props
Puppets and other props are important tools for children's programming. These items build interest and grab the children's attention. If you are on a limited budget, homemade puppets and toys can help you fill this need. If you are not handy with crafts, this is another opportunity to recruit some volunteers! There are many talented people who like to make things. This kind of assignment is usually welcomed because it has distinct parameters and is not open-ended as some others are. Many print sources are available that give directions, patterns, and suggestions. Here are a few that are especially helpful.

Martin, Sidney and Dana McMulan. *Puppets and Costumes.* New York: Monday Morning, 1986.

Morton, Brenda. *Soft Toys Made Easy.* New York: Taplinger Publishing Company, 1972.

Ross Laura. *Finger Puppets: Easy to Make, Fun to Use.* New York: Lathrop, Lee, Shepard, 1971.

Warrell, Estelle. *Be a Puppeteer.* New York: Mc Graw Hill, 1969.

If your time is limited and money is not an issue, you may prefer ready-made materials. Many of these have the advantage of being replicas of the illustrations in the story books that you will be using. Here is a partial list of companies that stock such materials. Write for their catalogs.

R. Dankin Company, Inc.,
P.O. Box 7200
San Francisco, CA 94120-9977

Furry Folk Puppets
Fred Reedy and Associates
P.O. Box 174
West Suffield, CT 06093

Gaylord, Inc.,
Box 4901
Syracuse, NY 13221-4901

Highsmith Company
W. 5527 Highway 106
P.O. Box 800
Fort Atkinson, WI 53538-0800

Nancy Renfo Studios
P.O. Box 164226
Austin, TX 78716

Pyramid School Products
6510 N. 54th Street
Tampa, FL 33610-1994

RESOURCES FOR ADULTS

There is an incredible amount of information available on books, reading, and related activities. The following sources are ones that I have found most helpful. At first glance, it would appear that many of these are aimed at the librarian. Many, however, have been recommended by me to parents and teachers, and they, too, have found them appropriate and "just what they were looking for."

Bookfinder: *When Kids Need Books*, 4th ed. Circle Pines, MN: American Guidance, 1989.

Connor, Jane Gardner. *Children's Library Services Handbook*. Phoenix, AZ: Oryx Press, 1990.

Cullinan, Bernice, ed. *Children's Literature in the Reading Program*. Newark, Delaware: International Reading Association, 1987.

Gilbert, Labritta. *Do Touch: Instant, Easy, Hands-On Learning Experiences for Young Children*. Mt. Rainier, MD: Gryphon House, 1989.

Gillespie, J.T. and Naden, C.J. *Best Books for Children* (revised regularly). New Providence, NJ: R.R. Bowker.

Hearne, Betsy. *Choosing Books for Children: A Common Sense Guide*. New York: Delacorte, 1991.

Hendrick, J. *The Whole Child: Early Education for the Eighties*. Saint Louis, MO: Times, Mirror, 1984.

Lamme, L.L. *Growing Up Reading. Sharing the Joys of Reading With Your Child*. Washington, DC: Acropolis Books, 1985.

Lima, Carolyn W. *A to Zoo: Subject Access to Picture Books*. New Providence, NJ: R.R. Bowker, 1989.

Mac Cann, Donnarae. *Social Responsibility in Librarianship*. Jefferson, NC: McFarland, 1989.

Raines, Shirley and Robert J. Canady. *Story Stretchers: Activities to Expand Children's Favorite Books*. Mt. Rainer, MD: Gryphon House, 1989.

Schiller, Pam and Joan Rossano. *The Instant Curriculum*. Mt. Rainier, MD: Gryphon House, 1990.

Sutherland, Zena and May Hill Arbuthnot. *Children and Books*, 8th ed. New York: HarperCollins, 1991.

Trelease, Jim. *The New Read Aloud Handbook*. New York: Penguin, 1989.

RESOURCE MATERIALS ON DEVELOPING READING SKILLS

Beginning with Excellence: An Adult Guide to Great Children's Reading. Boston: Sound Advantage Audio Publications, 1988. (audiocassettes).

Bunting, Eve. *The Wednesday Surprise*. New York: Clarion, 1989.

Butler, Dorothy. *Babies Need Books*. New York: Atheneum, 1985.

Cascardi, Andrea. *Good Books To Grow On: A Guide to Building Your Child's Library from Birth to Age Five*. New York: Warner Books, 1985.

Jones, Claudia. *Parents Are Teachers, Too*. Charlotte, VT: Williamson Publishing Company, 1988.

Kaye, Peggy. *Games For Reading*. New York: Pantheon Books, 1984.

Kircher, Audrey. *Basic Beginnings: A Handbook of Learning Games*. Philadelphia: Acropolis Books, 1985.

Larrick, Nancy. *A Parent's Guide to Children's Reading*, 5th ed. Louisville, KY: Westminster Press, 1982.

Mathews, Virginia, Judith G. Flum and Karen A. Whitney. "Kids Need Libraries." In *School Library Journal* 36:4 (April 1990): 33-37.

McCure, Lois. *Learning Through All Five Senses*. Mt. Rainer: Gryphon House, 1983.

Monsour, Margaret. "Libraries and Literacy: A Natural Connection." In *School Library Journal* 37:2 (February 1991): 33-37.

Parenting Strategies for Assessing Schools: Three A's for Professionals and At Risk Families. Moderated by Michael Fox, Pittsburgh: WQED Communications, 1989.

Pellowski, Anne. *Family Storytelling Handbook*. New York: Macmillan, 1987.

Preschool Services And Parent Education Committee, LASC. *First Steps to Literacy*. Chicago: American Library Association, 1990.

Talon, Carole. "Family Literacy: Libraries Doing What Libraries Do Best." In *Wilson Library Bulletin* 65:3 (November 1990): 30-34.

Trelease, Jim. *Hey Listen to This*. New York: Viking, 1992.

———. *New Read Aloud Handbook*, 2d ed. New York: Penguin Books, 1989.

U.S. Department of Education, *Youth Indicators, 1991*. Washington, DC: U.S. Government Printing Office, 1991.

RESOURCES FOR FINDING ALLIANCES AND PARTNERS

In addition to the directions given in chapter 3, these are some national organizations (there are many others) who may be able to help you. They can tell you if there is a local chapter to assist you directly, or may be able to make recommendations about other groups who can help.

Associations of Child Advocates
P.O. Box 5873
Cleveland, OH 44101
216-881-2225

Children's Foundation
815 15th St. N.W. Suite 928
Washington, DC 20005
202-347-3300

Foster Grandparents
1110 Vermont Ave. N.W. 6th Floor
Washington, DC 20525
202-634-9349

Lauchback Literacy Action
P.O. Box 131
Syracuse, NY 13210
315-442-9121

Literacy Volunteers of America
5795 Widgewaters Parkway
Syracuse, NY 13214
315-445-8000

National Association for the Education of Young Children
1834 Connecticut Ave. N.W.
Washington, DC 20009-5786
202-232-8777

National Association for Family Day Care
725 15th St. N.W., Suite 505
Washington, DC 20005
202-347-3356

National Head Start Association
1220 King Street Suite 200
Alexandria, VA 22314
703-739-0875

BIBLIOGRAPHY

Allen, Adele. *Library Services for Hispanic Children*. Phoenix: Oryx Press, 1987.

America 2000: An Education Strategy. Washington, DC: U.S. Department of Education, 1991.

American Library Association. *ALA Handbook of Organization, 1991-1992*. Chicago: American Library Association, 1991.

————. *First Steps to Literacy*. Chicago: American Library Association, 1990.

Anderson, Richard. Washington, DC: National Institute of Education.

Association for Library Service to Children. *Competencies for Librarians Serving Children in the Public Library*. Chicago: American Library Association, 1989.

Baker, Augusta. *Storytelling Art and Technique*. New York: R.R. Bowker, 1987.

Bloss, Meredith. "Take a Giant Step." In *Library Journal* 91:2 (Jan. 15, 1966): 324-336.

Ferguson, Lana H. and Sue Ellen C. Croteau. *Building Blocks: An Annotated Bibliography for Day Care Providers Serving Children Ages 2 Through 5*. Guildford, CT: Guildford Free Library, 1991.

Flanagan, Joan. *The Grass Roots Fund-Raising Book*. Chicago: Contemporary Books, 1982.

Glazier, Suzanne. "Who's Non-Verbal?" In *Library Journal* 91:2 (Jan. 15, 1966): 341-43.

Kotler, Philip. *Strategic Marketing for Non-Profit Organizations*. Englewood Cliffs, NJ: Prentice-Hall, 1987.

Laughlin, Mildred, and Watt Letty. *Developing Learning Skills Through Children's Literature*. Phoenix: Oryx, 1986.

Levinson, Nancy Smiler. *Clara and the Bookwagon*. New York: Harper and Row, 1988.

McClure, Charles, *et al. Planning and Role Setting for Public Libraries*. Chicago: American Library Association, 1987.

MacDonald, Margaret Read. *Booksharing*. Hamden, CT: The Shoe String Press. 1988

Mathews, Virginia H., Judith G. Flum and Karen Whitney. "Kids Need Libraries." In *School Library Journal* 36:4 (April 1990).

Olson, Stan, ed. *The Foundation Directory*, 13th ed. New York: Foundation Center, 1991.

Rollock, Barbara T. *Public Library Services for Children*. Hamden, CT: Shoe String Press, 1988.

Sutherland, Tina. *Children and Books*. New York: HarperCollins, 1991.

Youth Indicators 1991. Washington, DC: National Center for Education Statistics, 1991.

INDEX

Marcia Trotta is the Assistant Director of The Meriden Public Library in Connecticut. She previously was their Director of Children's Services. Trotta is the immediate past president of the Connecticut State Library and was chosen as the Outstanding Librarian by the Connecticut Library Association in 1986 and again in 1993. She is also an Adjunct Professor at the School of Library Science and Information Technology at Southern Connecticut State University.